D1328404

What's in a Name?

What's in a Name?

Reflections on Language,
Magic, and Religion

G.A. Wells

OPEN  COURT

Chicago and La Salle, Illinois

OPEN COURT and the above logo are registered in the U.S. Patent and Trademark Office.

© 1993 by Open Court Publishing Company

First printing 1993

Printed and bound in the United States of America.

Library of Congress Cataloging-in-Publication Data

Wells, George Albert, 1926-
    What's in a name? : reflections on language, magic, and religion / G.A. Wells.
      p. cm.
    Includes bibliographical references and index.
    ISBN 0-8126-9238-1. — ISBN 0-8126-9239-X (pbk.)
    1. Language and languages—Philosophy. 2. Thought and thinking. 3. Magic. 4. Religion—Controversial literature. I. Title.
    P106.W328 1993
    401—dc20   93-28907
                                                          CIP

Contents

Preface

Among uncivilized peoples, the belief is found (so Frazer tells us in *The Golden Bough*) that eating timid or ugly animals will make one timid or ugly. This idea that abstract qualities such as timidity or ugliness can be conveyed from one creature to another may well have been encouraged by the use of nouns to designate them, thus making it possible to talk of them as one does of concrete objects.

The opinions criticized in this book suggest that the relation between words, ideas, and things is often little better understood even today. My illustrations will show that atheists can in this regard be as much astray as religious apologists.

The nature of an idea, its relation to reality, and the way in which language serves to express ideas—all this is not merely of academic interest, but of fundamental practical importance. How language originated is a theoretical question of restricted interest, although the origin of the instrument is not entirely irrelevant to the question of its proper use. But the insecure connection between words and ideas is something that bedevils all reasoning that is not closely related to practical and experimental matters.

Most of the writers discussed in my two opening chapters exaggerate the importance of language—either at the expense of things or at the expense of ideas. In my first chapter I discuss A.J. Ayer's *Language, Truth and Logic,* where he was afraid of raising what he thought would be insoluble metaphysical problems if he talked about things instead of 'sensations', and where he regarded the philosopher as a kind of arbitrator on the conventions of language whose business it is to study its rules and provide definitions which have nothing to do with empirical facts. The second edition of this book was immensely successful. Ayer himself recorded in 1986 that a new impression of it appeared almost annually for 25 years after its publication in 1946, that it was translated into a dozen foreign languages and "still maintains a steady sale in paperback both in England and in the United States" ('My Mental Development', in *The Philosophy of A.J. Ayer,* edited by L.E. Hahn, La Salle: Open Court, 1992, pp. 18–19). Hence, however much Ayer later modified his views—a fact of which I take due cognizance—he is, in virtue of this book, responsible for some of the strange ideas about language that have since become current. As he himself has said, in the context already quoted, the book "served as a springboard for the development of at least some variants of what came to be known as linguistic philosophy."

If Ayer was unwilling to commit himself to talking about things, the behaviorists positively jettisoned ideas and made thinking into merely talking (to others or to oneself). Some of those who oppose them, while not always committing themselves definitively on the question of ideas or 'concepts', clearly wish to manage without them. This, as I show in my second chapter, leaves the whole psychology of reasoning in the hands of the grammarians: their analysis of language becomes the analysis of mind; hence the importance that has come to be ascribed to linguistics.

Of these two initial chapters, the first is a fuller treatment of matters adumbrated in Chapter 1 of my *Belief and Make-Believe* (Open Court, 1991). I have done my best not to make undue demands on readers, but they may well find the going easier from the beginning of Chapter 2. I envisage readers of general education, and am not presupposing any specialist knowledge.

The argument of Chapter 3 (on magic) is that magical ideas derive from plausible errors in communicative practices—errors concerning the real efficacy of gestures and words—and have survived in a time when the errors have been exposed. The errors, it is argued, arose from extending beyond their proper scope generalizations based on accurate observations—a common source of human, indeed of mammalian error. Apart from magical practices, human behaviour falls into five chief categories: i. involuntary reflex or instinctive movements adapted to special situations or bodily conditions; ii. expressive actions (such as weeping, laughing, shouting) prompted by strong emotion but not closely adapted to circumstances; iii. play, that is to say behaviour which has no particular end in view, but is indulged in for its own sake; iv. practical behaviour, such as building or cooking, suitably adapted to intelligible aims; and v. communication—a form of practical behaviour that deserves a special category because of its significance. My argument is that magic is practical in intention, but ill-conceived and ineffectual, and that while the fallacy of prayer lies in its being addressed to imaginary beings, the fallacy of magic lies in ascribing to gestures and to words an imaginary power. Here I am controverting the not uncommon view that magic is merely expressive—an expression of strong wishes with no expectation of their fulfilment. Such an assessment of magic is typical of the tendency to stress emotional determinants of human behaviour at the expense of intellectual ones, and to look askance at any suggestion that what people do (particularly what uncivilized people do) is influenced to any great extent by their beliefs.

The first three sections of Chapter 4 discuss i. attempts to represent the language of the Bible as of a special kind; ii. the appeal of biblical commentators to certain theories of literary criticism, according to which any work of literature can include a great multiplicity of meanings (If this is so, we may choose those which we find convenient.); iii. incoherent apologists whose arguments are based primarily on verbal associations; and iv. attempts to represent biblical narratives as intrinsically meaningful, whether or not the events they record occurred or not. In all four areas, misconceptions about language are involved, and one's estimate of the value of the Bible is not likely to be enhanced by the apparent need to vindicate it by means of a variety of approaches that are flawed in this way.

The final section of Chapter 4, and also the

final part of the previous section, illustrate, from the frank admissions of a number of eminent theologians, how difficult religious defence of the Bible has become. These theologians do not (as do so many of their colleagues) surrender the old dogmas only to replace them with barely intelligible philosophemes. They honestly admit to uncertainty, and they are now sufficiently numerous among those within Christianity who have real and detailed acquaintance with the Bible to make simple discounting of their voices inappropriate. I am not saying that the relevant issues are to be settled by their—or anyone's else's—authority. But when a substantial number of the most serious investigators reach conclusions inimicable to their Holy Orders (and/or professional positions), their arguments are not to be ignored.

The final chapter outlines some characteristics of man which make him much more liable to far-reaching misconceptions and to misbehaviour than are other mammals. The fundamental instincts and emotions are much the same in man and in other social animals. The apparent difference arises because the development of the human brain makes possible an enormous increase of situations and reactions linked to these instincts. The aggressive instinct of the wolf or pig can find outlet in but a small variety of reactions, and the situations which elicit the emotion are fairly uniform. But the human brain facilitates thousands of variations on this theme. Moreover, the development of language has, apart from its co-ordinating function in society, abridged certain processes of thinking and so speeded up invention, but it has also been a fruitful source of new confusions. In his book *On Human Nature*

(Cambridge (Mass.): Harvard University Press, 1978), Edward O. Wilson castigates those who naively suppose that "science and learning will banish religion", and that "humanity migrates toward knowledge by logotaxis, an automatic orientation toward information" (p. 169). No one who understood what is involved in forming adequate ideas on matters of any complexity could possibly subscribe to such a position. Yet Wilson may well be right in supposing that, regrettably, it is a not uncommon standpoint among sceptics. Quite apart from intellectual difficulties in forming reliable ideas, there are also emotional factors which—often perniciously—influence ideas and beliefs, and this too is given some attention in my final chapter.

As an undergraduate in the 1940s, I became suspicious of much that passes for literary comment and criticism, and came to think that a misuse of language is often involved. Wider study has convinced me that the same is true of a great deal that is written in defence of religious and philosophical ideas. I was lucky to have a good deal of stimulus and guidance from my teacher, the late F.R.H. Englefield, and from another of his pupils, David Oppenheimer, who died in 1991. Another close friend and helper, Carl Lofmark, also died, tragically prematurely, in 1991. I owe much to all three. I am grateful too to Mr Daniel O'Hara for his helpful comments on a draft of my manuscript. Finally, I thank my former secretary, Mrs Evelyn Stone, for her willingness, in retirement, to continue with her careful typing of my manuscripts.

1
Words, Ideas, and Things

I. Introduction

When we first learn to speak and to understand, we are surrounded by people who make noises and also by a great variety of other happenings. Gradually we learn that the apparent chaos of our environment is not quite chaotic, that there are certain recurrent sequences, certain constant groupings, that one event is correlated with another, and that from observation of the one we may confidently look forward to observation of the other. Animals do as much. The dog, hearing his master's voice, expects to see his master; scenting his dinner, he expects to see and taste it. Reaching the gate, he expects to find the garden path beyond. Amidst a multitude of disconnected and uninteresting phenomena—sights, smells, and pressures—he discerns a certain constant distribution in time and space, correlation between situations. He learns to recognize those which are of special significance to him.

Human science simply carries these processes further. A scientific law is no more than a formula purporting to state how different observable phenomena are related in time and space. In short, we learn to construct in our minds an organized world. No religious commitments are involved, even though apologists have claimed that belief in order logically implies a deity responsible for the order, whether or not the individual accepts such implication. A.E. Taylor, for instance, declares:

> The conception of God as perfect and flawless intelligence is manifestly the source of our rooted belief in the presence of intelligible order and system throughout nature; it has created the intellectual temper from which modern science itself has arisen.[1]

Presumably by 'nature' we are to understand the whole universe and everything which goes on in it. If so, we must say that it is certainly not completely orderly. There may be order and uniformities to be discovered in it, but there is a great deal of chaos. The uniform sequence of day and night such as is experienced approximately at the equator, the uniform properties of water under more or less definable conditions, the uniform behaviour of the river Nile—these are familiar examples of uniformity, and the meaning is that certain observable and measurable events recur. The biological view of inferences drawn from uniformities is that animals are affected by their experiences in such a way that their reaction to a repeated experience is different from their reaction to the first. When a situation is repeated many times, the behaviour of the animal becomes adapted to it, provided that it has some significance for him in relation to his way of life. If human beings have observed many more regularities in the world than dogs, it is because their interests are more extensive, not because they believe—or ought logically to believe—in God.

That any object or situation may be interpreted as involving or implying some other object or situation not immediately perceptible is a fact only remotely connected with communication, although it underlies all intelligent behaviour, communication included. We draw inferences from someone's words in the same way that we draw inferences from the screech of brakes, the howl of the wind, or the crow of the cock, and experience teaches us what inferences to draw.

Bertrand Russell tries to explain, in terms of visible behaviour, the process of understanding a word. "You understand the word 'fox'", he says, "if, when you hear it you have an impulse to act in a manner appropriate to the presence of a fox, and when you see a fox, you have an impulse to say 'fox'".[2] So I understand the word 'tiger' if, on hearing it, I have an impulse to act as I should if I met one in the garden. In fact, of course, when an animal learns the significance of a sign—whether this be a word, or any sound, smell, or sight—he acts in a manner which prepares him for the anticipated situation as soon as it is presented. There may be common components in the two reactions, but as a rule the response to the sign is quite different from the response to the situation itself. If the baby felt impelled to react to the word 'milk' as it does to the substance 'milk', it would have an urge to drink the word.

My quotation shows that Russell also supposes that the appearance of something impels
the person who sees it to utter its name. I am
surrounded by all kinds of objects in my room,
making use of them in turn as I have occasion, but
I do not have the smallest tendency to name them
when I handle them. Some people talk to themselves when they are alone, but more often about
what is going on in their imagination than about
things present. Russell's supposition betrays his
sympathy with behaviorism which, as we shall
see, makes thinking little (if anything) more than
talking. His whole discussion of words, ideas, and
things is almost inextricably muddled. In his
History of Western Philosophy (London: Allen and
Unwin, 1946) he suggests that meaningful words
must imply the existence of corresponding
things: because general words have a meaning,
there must, he supposes, be general things or
"universals"; for "general words . . . are not
meaningless noises, and it is difficult to see how
they can have a meaning if the world consists
entirely of particular things, such as are designated by proper names" (p. 148). On similar
grounds one might argue that, because the words
'without' and 'notwithstanding' have a meaning,
there must therefore exist somewhere in the
universe realities corresponding to them.
Russell's discussion of 'particular things designated by proper names' is equally unhelpful. He
thinks it "fairly obvious that proper names owe
their existence in ordinary language to the concept of 'substance'— . . . a substance or entity is
named, and then properties are assigned to it";
and as "most of us, nowadays, do not accept
'substance' as a useful notion", and as "proper
names . . . are ghosts of substances", it might be

desirable to "adopt in philosophy a language without proper names" (1948, pp. 87–88). But was the river Thames named because it was regarded as a substance? Its material content is ever changing, and even its form changes. It is nevertheless useful to have a name for it.

Russell's arguments fail to distinguish between the meaning of a *word* and the meaning of a *thing*. The meaning of a word may be the thing it denotes, but it may be merely the ideas associated with the word in someone's mind. The meaning of a thing is its significance for somebody, what it implies, leads him to expect, or causes him to remember. The meaning of Friday's footprint to Robinson Crusoe was that he was not alone on the island. The meanings of the things 'salt' and 'sugar' are, for most people, complexes of culinary or gastronomic associations. The meanings of the corresponding words are either the typical materials found in grocers' shops, or the notions, more or less abstract, derived from these materials. Thus the meaning of a word is either the thing it denotes or the ideas it connotes, but the meaning of a thing is all the other things which we have learned to connect with it.

It is not hard to know what a word is, whether we regard it as a noise which affects the ear, or as a muscular effort of the vocal organs, but it is much less easy to find agreement on the subject of ideas and thinking. It is sometimes supposed that some logical process, in particular inference, must be involved in thinking. But it is surely a thought process when one merely pictures to oneself a scene or a face, or performs in imagination a gymnastic exercise.

Nothing is gained here by substituting technical terms. If we cannot clarify the relation between words, ideas, and things with the aid of common language, we certainly cannot do so by talking, in the manner of Ogden and Richards, about 'symbols', 'references', and 'referents'.[3] Perhaps someone has the idea of something he has found and gives it a name. If he wishes someone else to form the same idea, his best method will be, if possible, to show him the thing. Otherwise he can describe it in words, comparing it with things that are more usual and familiar, and referring to special distinguishing features. But whatever words he uses will serve his purpose only if they are known to the other person, and if the latter has learned to associate them with the same *things*. If I cannot produce a spade for exhibition and wish to convey the idea of one to someone who has never seen or heard of such a thing, I can do so by speaking of wood, iron, handle, and so forth, provided that he has already learned these words through association with real things. When a child who has never seen a giraffe, on hearing the name for the first time asks what it means, we attempt to build up in his mind some kind of picture which resembles that which we have in ours; and we do this by reference to objects with which he is supposed to be already familiar. It is a large animal. That at once suggests a horse, a cow, or an elephant. It is yellow with black spots. Many objects are already known of this colour and design. It has a very long neck. Since the animals already known have necks of varying length, there is no difficulty in imagining this particular feature, at least vaguely. A drawing will, of course, be much more effective than any verbal description.

If the questioner is not a child, he may be told that a giraffe is an even-toed ungulate characterized by the great length of the cervical vertebrae, by bony prominences on the frontal bones which become fused with the skull, by orbits which are completely encircled by bone, without lachrymal fossa, by an absence of canines in the upper jaw, and so on. The object of such a zoological specification is to place the animal in the systematic series and to show its affinities. It assumes that the animal and its conspicuous characters are well-known, and emphasizes rather those features which are of systematic significance, and which are known to the questioner from other—real, not purely verbal—contexts.

The relative effectiveness of description by means of words and by means of drawings or paintings can be illustrated by the following mental experiment: think of an animal just over two feet in length, standing about 14 inches high on four legs, and possessing a tail and a brown body, except for black patches behind the ears and on the forelimbs. This list of details could be considerably prolonged, but already difficulty will be felt in retaining them all. If, however, instead of such a verbal description, a picture of a fox is shown, then they can all be seen at one glance. On the other hand, think of the following: a fox trots along a path, jumps a garden fence, approaches a chicken run, digs a hole under the wire, and slips through it. To envisage all this is easy because the words indicate a sequence of actions, not co-existing things or co-existing parts of one thing. A painting could portray only one particular moment in this sequence.

It is a particular aspect of a thing that is capable of the most lively mental representation. If, for instance, we call a dog into memory, we recall some aspect of him as he appears to us in a certain environment: we envisage him lying in his usual place, or we hear him barking at the door, or feel him tugging at our coat. It is therefore not by systematic description of the concrete thing, but by a quick suggestion of some familiar aspect of it that words can produce lively conceptions of it in a listener's mind. In an essay entitled 'The Philosophy of Style' (included in the second of the two volumes of essays he published in 1868), Herbert Spencer well summarized the requirements of effectiveness as "abridging the description" by selection of "typical elements which carry many others along with them". To illustrate what he had in mind, he quoted from Tennyson's 'Mariana':

> All day within the dreamy house,
> The doors upon their hinges creaked;
> The blue fly sung in the pane; the mouse
> Behind the mouldering wainscot shrieked,
> Or from the crevice peered about.

He commented:

> Our attention is rarely drawn by the buzzing of a fly in the window, save when everything is still. While the inmates are moving about the house, mice usually keep silent; and it is only when extreme quietness reigns that they peep from their retreats. Hence each of the facts mentioned, presupposing numerous others, calls up these with more or less distinctness; and revives the feeling of dull solitude with which they are connected in our experience. Were all these facts detailed instead of suggested, the attention would be so frittered away that little impression of dreariness would be produced. Similarly in

other cases. Whatever the nature of the thought to be conveyed, this skilful selection of a few particulars which imply the rest, is the key to success.

It is of note too that, although Tennyson lists co-existent phenomena, each one of them is an activity: the doors creak, the fly sings, and so on.

II. Locke

If Russell at times writes as though meaningful words must stand for things, and not merely for ideas, the opposite position—that words can represent only ideas—is also responsible for much confusion. The truth surely is that words can serve the purpose of communication between people who use the same words for the same things. 'Frog' is the name of a familiar animal, and different people have different ideas about it. If we pretend that the name always stands for the idea rather than the thing, then communication would be possible only between persons who happened to have the same idea. A physiologist's idea of a frog is hardly likely to be identical with mine, but when he speaks the word to me, it awakens my idea. By reference to a real frog we may both correct and elaborate our ideas and make them more alike.

Locke is among those who insist that the word does not represent the thing, but only the idea in the user's mind. It would follow that, if two people use the same word in the belief that they are using it in reference to one and the same thing, they are deluded, for each in fact uses it in reference to his own idea of that thing:

> Because men would not be thought to talk barely of their own imaginations, but of things as really they are, . . . they often suppose their words to stand also for the reality of things . . . [But] it is perverting the use of words . . . whenever we make them stand for any thing but those ideas we have in our own minds.[4]

It is true that the memory of a word can be linked only to the memory of a thing, which is to say: to an idea. But this idea is ultimately derived from experience of a real thing; and it is only because two persons may form ideas from the same or similar things that they can get similar ideas and meaningfully use the same name for them. Admittedly, difference in idea may lead to misunderstanding and is therefore important. But if it were true that the word stood simply and solely for the idea in the mind of the speaker, then the meaning of the word will change as fast as he enlarges his idea of the thing; and it seems misleading to say that he no longer means the same by the name when he learns more about the thing. When a child says he can see a frog, the naturalist may well accept his word; and his idea is connected with the child's by the thing which is common to the experience of both. It is very often not someone's ideas that I am concerned to know, but the facts. When someone says it is raining, I know what to expect, whether the speaker is an experienced meteorologist or an ignoramus.

Locke was led to say that the words represent only the ideas in the user's mind probably because he was thinking of those words which do not directly represent any material thing or process—in particular of the empty words of philosophy which indeed have no meaning except what lurks in the mind of the speaker. The fault lies here in the wrong supposition that there is something which corresponds to the idea. But as long as the idea represents anything in nature which all people may become acquainted with, then the word can be attached to this thing, and cannot in fact be attached by the community at large to anything else.

Locke may also have been led to the view he takes because he had in mind questions which can be answered only with the aid of an arbitrary definition of the relevant words, for instance: "when a man asks whether this or that thing he sees, let it be a drill [a baboon] or a monstrous foetus be a man or no" (3:10:21). But there are also questions like: are fossil marsupials found in Europe? Is there a gorilla in the London Zoo? Here, the words are sufficiently well understood in terms of material things, and these questions do not call for special *ad hoc* definitions. Persons who raise or answer such questions are in agreement about the meaning of the words—in terms of real experiences, and not merely other words. Locke is well aware of the futility of trying to define verbally words whose meaning can be obtained directly from experience:

> If anyone asks me what this solidity is, I send him to his senses to inform him: let him put a flint or a football between his hands and then endeavour to join them, and he will know. . . . The simple ideas we have are such as experience teaches them us; but if, beyond that, we endeavour by words to make them

clearer in the mind, we shall succeed no
better than if we went about to clear up the
darkness of a blind man's mind by talking,
and to discourse into him the ideas of light
and colour (2:4:6).

But because we do not require a verbal definition
of solidity to know what we are talking about, this
does not mean that we know all that there is to
know about it simply because we understand the
word.

Naturally enough, Locke was not able to sustain the view that words can be given only to
ideas; for ideas represent things, and in the
following passage about words which stand for
general ideas he passes from the idea to the thing
and back again as if there were little or no
difference between them (I have added the italics):

It is not enough for the perfection of language that sounds can be made signs of *ideas*
unless those signs can so be made use of as to
comprehend several particular *things;* for the
multiplication of words would have perplexed their use, had every particular *thing*
need of a distinct name to be signified by. To
remedy this inconvenience, language had yet
a farther improvement in the use of general
terms, whereby one word was made to mark a
multitude of particular *existences;* which ad-
vantageous use of sounds was obtained only
by the difference of the *ideas* they were made
signs of: those names becoming general
which are made to stand for general ideas,
and those remaining particular where the
ideas they are used for are particular (3:1:3).

Locke, then, in sometimes confusing ideas and
things, betrays that he only partly understood the

relation between these and words. This is not surprising, as so many writers today are still muddled about it.

III. Ayer

a. Philosophy and Language
A.J. Ayer's book *Language, Truth and Logic,* first published in 1936, and still in print over 50 years later, bears some responsibility for the exaggeration of the importance of language that is so widespread today.[5] According to him, the philosopher is a kind of arbitrator on the conventions of language whose business it is to study its rules and to provide definitions which have nothing to do with empirical facts.[6] I shall have to quote him at some length in the course of commenting on his strange views and uncovering what motivates them. If this presents my readers with some arid passages, I can only say that it is the prevalence of philosophizing of this kind which shows how wrong it would be to assume that the more commonsense positions which I am defending are so obvious as to be generally appreciated and accepted. Indeed, I shall be able to show that Ayer and some others akin to him have prompted a strong religious reaction which is as wide of common sense as anything in him and his like. The need for sobriety on the relevant matters is best appreciated if one is first aware of the wide range of indefensible views on them that have recently been, and to some extent still are, so popular.

Ayer seems to assume that, in any set of

symbols, such as language, a number of permissible transformations—substitutions of one word or sentence for another—are included, and that logic is concerned with investigating the possible combinations of these transformations. The following passage illustrates what he has in mind, and is also a typical specimen of his style, in that it aims to create an impression of remorseless pursuit of a problem:

> We define a symbol *explicitly* when we put forward another symbol, or symbolic expression which is synonymous with it. And the word 'synonymous' is here used in such a way that two symbols belonging to the same language can be said to be synonymous if, and only if, the simple substitution of one symbol for the other, in any sentence in which either can significantly occur, always yields a new sentence which is equivalent to the old. And we say that two sentences of the same language are equivalent if, and only if, every sentence which is entailed by any given group of sentences in conjunction with one of them is entailed by the same group in conjunction with the other. And, in this usage of the word 'entail', a sentence *s* is said to entail a sentence *t* when the proposition expressed by *t* is deducible from the proposition expressed by *s;* while a proposition *p* is said to be deducible from, or to follow from, a proposition *q* when the denial of *p* contradicts the assertion of *q.* (pp. 59–60)

The reader's first impression is probably that this analysis is exhaustive and final; the term 'synonymous' is defined in terms of 'equivalence', 'equivalence' in terms of 'entail', 'entail' in terms of 'deduce', and 'deduce' finally in terms of 'denial' and 'contradiction'. In fact, however, there are other words in these definitions which require explaining at least as much as these: for example 'symbol', 'proposition', 'significant', 'express'. But what, after all, is gained by this definition of one word in terms of another equally ambiguous? One might go on thus substituting one for another as long as the dictionary furnished fresh vocables, without clarifying the original one. For Ayer, however, the whole business of philosophical ratiocination consists in commutations and substitutions of agglomerations of 'symbols', so that he does not feel any obligation to produce anything at the conclusion of the operation but a new verbal formula. It is true that his phrase "the simple substitution of one symbol for the other in any sentence in which either can significantly occur" does seem, at first sight, to imply that a phrase or verbal expression must have a meaning. But when we ask how the meaning can be ascertained, we are given only the rules according to which one sentence may be replaced by another. Again, when he speaks of a proposition being "expressed by" a sentence he seems to suggest a distinction between the verbal formula, the 'sentence', and its thinkable content, the proposition. But as he strenuously denies that the propositions in question have any factual content, we must suppose that a proposition differs only in form from a sentence.

So far, we have been dealing with what Ayer calls "explicit" definitions, which he distinguishes from "definitions in use". He writes, apropos of the latter:

> We define a symbol *in use,* not by saying that it is synonymous with some other symbol, but by showing how sentences in which it significantly occurs can be translated into equiva-

lent sentences, which contain neither the *definiendum* itself, nor any of its synonyms. (p. 60)

Here again, then, it is only a matter of putting one formula instead of another. It is hard to discern any significant difference between the two cases. A sentence is only a collection of symbols and therefore only a rather more complex symbol, so that the first type of definition deals with the replacement of elementary symbols, and the second with that of more complex ones.

As an example of 'equivalence', we may take the definition which Ayer gives of "causal connection":

> Every general proposition of the form 'C causes E' is equivalent to a proposition of the form 'whenever C then E', where the symbol 'whenever' must be taken to refer, not to a finite number of actual instances of C, but to the infinite number of possible instances. (p. 55)

Now if the substitution of the second formula for the first is but an arbitrary prescription with no "factual" reference, nobody can challenge it; but then it is devoid of interest. If, however, the substitution is supposed to be valid for real events, then it becomes essential to ask what the words are intended to stand for. Thus, if the word 'cause' is used in its customary sense the transformation is clearly inadmissible. The propositions 'mosquitos cause malaria', 'lobsters cause indigestion', 'bombs cause destruction' are perfectly intelligible and, in their normal acceptation, valid. But if we transform them in accordance with Ayer's formula we get: 'whenever mosquitos then malaria', 'whenever lobsters, then indigestion', and so on, and these are evidently not valid. If, on the other hand, we stipulate that C must include *all* the conditions of E, the conversion will stand, but we shall have to define 'causes' as meaning 'denotes all the conditions of'.

It is absurd to suppose that simple rules for conversion like this can be constructed for ordinary language; for where we are using words and not mathematical symbols, the meaning is very rarely sufficiently precise and unambiguous to make such simple statements as 'C causes E' more than locally and temporarily valid. Alternative ways of making such a statement are useful because one form is sometimes more appropriate in one set of circumstances and another in another. Words give rise to ideas, and, where the same word gives rise to a number of different ideas, the situation or context suffices as a rule to eliminate the inappropriate associations. Where genuine misunderstanding does occur the best remedy is a reference not to more words, but to real things. If all definitions were really only verbal substitutes, no child could ever learn to use a language, that is, to associate words with objects and actions. As we saw, once a large stock of words has been already acquired, the use of a new word may be learned with the aid of a verbal definition. But the latter always depends, directly or indirectly, on learning by what teachers of language call the 'direct method', and no definition can be more than empty verbiage if its terms do not rest ultimately on the experience of real things and events.

In Ayer's view, the true philosopher restricts himself to tautologies, which he also calls *'a priori* propositions', 'analytical propositions', or 'linguistic propositions'. He says that "a proposition is analytic when its validity depends solely on the definitions of the symbols it contains, and synthetic when its validity is determined by the facts of experience" (p. 78). In normal usage a tautology means saying the same things twice over in different words, as Fowler illustrates in his Dictionary with the sentence: "They arrived one after the other in succession". What Ayer means by a tautology is a statement of an arbitrary equivalence between symbols. He holds that the validity of such propositions is independent both of the external world and of our minds (pp. 84, 87). Against this I would urge that the validity of any proposition depends on 1. what we mean by it, and 2. what is the fact; and that it depends therefore both on our minds and on the external world.

Belief in the mysterious power of words—in spells, for instance—is a familiar form of magic. Ayer appears to believe in a still more mysterious power that resides, not in the language itself, but in some superior insight of the philosopher which enables him, from the purely arbitrary relations between linguistic forms, to deduce the validity of scientific conclusions. "We may look to the philosopher", he says, "to show us what we accept as constituting sufficient evidence for the truth of any given empirical proposition" (pp. 48–49). He holds that the propositions which concern the philosopher are so entirely devoid of any relation to matters of fact that no contradiction between them and any proposition of science is even conceivable, and that "this makes it clear that the possibility of philosophical analysis is independent of any empirical assumptions" (p. 57). This independence is evidently a matter of considerable importance, for it enables the philosopher to carry on his work without having to pay attention to the observations and discoveries of science. The scientist, however, must seek the philosopher's approval for all his generalizations, for, as we saw, it is the philosopher who tells us what is sufficient evidence for the truth of any empirical proposition, and so the philosopher keeps the whip hand. In some mysterious way, from the scrutiny of linguistic formulas and study of their arbitrarily ordained equivalences, he becomes qualified to adjudicate on the validity of scientific conclusions!

It is obvious from all this that one reason for Ayer's strange views is a certain concern to boost the importance of philosophy. Reasoning processes, whether effective or not, are prompted by some kind of desire, aim, or motive, and the separation of intellect and emotion, of the mind and the passions, which was long taken for granted, is no longer tenable. Reasoning cannot begin without some kind of nervous stimulation; and cannot be long sustained without a strong emotional driving force. Where the process terminates in a practical decision, we can often infer the motive from the act. Now it is today much harder than of yore for philosophers to justify their activities. Formerly they concerned themselves with such questions as the structure of the universe, the constitution of matter, the nature of the human mind, and the individual's relation to society. All these topics now come within the competence of recognized branches of science—astronomy, physics, psychology, and sociology. History tells of philosophers who questioned the reality of the universe, who even doubted their own existence; but they do not readily doubt the importance of philosophy. One purpose of Ayer's book is evidently to establish that there is in fact something important for them to do.

I will attempt to summarize. If the philosopher is really restricted to propositions about language, to definitions and inferences from definitions, and is debarred from making use of experimental facts, then it is not possible that he should make any contribution to knowledge. One may find many equivalent verbal formulas, but one must go back to concrete examples in order to understand what is meant. One cannot attach belief to any arbitrary collection of sounds or noises, still less derive thence belief in another equally arbitrary collection. We may say that one symbol is equivalent to another, but the word 'equivalence' can have no meaning if the symbols have none. All our definitions are, in the last resort, in terms of things, and it is the common material world which forms the medium by which we can exchange ideas.

b. 'Necessary' Truth

One reason why Ayer does not admit that definitions must rest ultimately on the experience of real things and events is his readiness to regard as true of language what he considers to be true of mathematics. Logicians are apt to suppose that they can define words as easily as they can mathematical functions. The fundamental mathematical symbols 1, 2, 3, 4, and so on have a meaning that is very little subject to misunderstanding, and the small number of elementary operations that can be performed with them may be described without much ambiguity. On this foundation, mathematics is built. The more complex symbols can always be defined in terms of the more elementary, and as these fundamentals are usually taken for granted, all mathematical definitions appear to consist in the substitution of one set of symbols for another. On this basis, Ayer argues (pp. 72–73) that mathematical propositions are tautologies. As we saw, he regards a tautology as a statement of an arbitrary equivalence between symbols, and he believes that it is quite independent of anything in the actual world (p. 87). That seven and five make twelve is, on this view, not a matter of experience, but a linguistic convention, just as convention makes 'oculist' synonymous with 'eye-doctor' (p. 85).

In later years, Ayer declared himself no longer so sure that statements in mathematics are true merely "by convention".[7] It is, however, a view that has appealed to mathematicians themselves. The Scottish philosopher and mathematician Dugald Stewart asserted that in mathematics we do not deal with facts but with inferences from definitions, and that whereas "in most other instances some previous discussion is necessary to show that the definitions which we lay down correspond with facts", in mathematics this is not the case. Simple arithmetical equations such as 2 + 2 = 4 are "mere definitions", and "it is from a few fundamental principles of this sort, or at least from principles which are essentially of the same description, that all the most complicated results in the science are derived".[8]

If this view of mathematics is correct, and if language is analogous to mathematics, then it is possible to hold that definitions in words involve recourse only to other words. It is, then, perhaps not surprising to find Stewart anticipating, in the following passage, the type of argument about language that we find in Ayer:

It appears that it might be possible, by devising a set of arbitrary definitions, to form a science which, although conversant about moral, political or physical ideas, should yet be as certain as geometry. It is of no moment whether the definitions assumed correspond with facts or not, provided they do not express impossibilities, and be not inconsistent with each other (p. 158).

To this, as to Ayer's similar reasoning, one must object: how can arbitrary definitions be judged consistent or inconsistent with each other? Two definitions can be inconsistent only if there is some real incompatibility between the things to which the definitions point. But, as we shall see in the next section of this chapter, Ayer was afraid of lapsing into metaphysics if he talked about concrete things.

Stewart refers with strong disapproval to the view that mathematics is really an inductive science.[9] He insists, as many philosophers do, that, since mathematical propositions are indubitable, they cannot rest on experience, which can at best establish only probability. He deprecates the use of mathematical demonstrations for what he allows to be experimental truths. It would, of course, be awkward if he had to admit such demonstrations, for to do so would put physics or mechanics on a level with mathematics, and it would then be hard to draw the distinction between mathematics and the rest of science which seems to him so important.

Ayer tries to substantiate his assertion that "the truths of formal logic and pure mathematics are necessarily true" by examining cases "in which they might be seen to be confuted". If, he says, what appears to be a Euclidean triangle is found by measurement not to have angles totalling 180 degrees, we do not abandon the relevant theorem (p. 75). Certainly there are hypotheses much more credible than that this well established belief should be unfounded. But if what appears to be a sample of hydrogen is found, on being subjected to the usual test, not to be inflammable, we do not say that after all hydrogen is an inert gas, for we know that, in view of our accumulated experience and knowledge of hydrogen, another hypothesis is preferable. What Ayer says of a mathematical truth is true of any well established generalization: "We always preserve its validity by adopting some other explanation of the occurrence" (p. 76).

Let us consider further what is characteristically involved in propositions the truth of which is independent of particular experiences. We may observe that this or that person is benefited by a certain treatment. On the other hand we may recognize a general principle, of which the observed cases are merely particular instances— namely the principle that this remedy is applicable to this disease, irrespective of who the invalid may be. Such generalizations are always guesses, and their formulation always involves an abstraction: the rule no longer applies to this or that individual, but to this or that quality, property, or condition, in no matter what individual it may be found. If a particular case seems to belie the rule, it is because the quality with which the rule is concerned is never found in isolation, and the rule may, in consequence, be masked by other conflicting rules. If no real triangle has angles which give the required sum, it is because we are never dealing with those properties that constitute a triangle unmixed with others that are not included in the definition.

Science makes continual use of these abstractions—the 'perfect gas', the 'incompressible liquid', 'continuous matter', 'infinite dilution', and so on. These notions are formed in the same way and perform the same functions in thought as the abstractions of mathematics. It is important to understand the difference between experimental data and such conceptual systems invented to hold them together. The perfect gas, the solution of infinite dilution are empirical ideas insofar as they are the result of interpolation or extrapolation. In the same way the propositions of geometry refer to ideal systems—simplified, idealized bodies composed of lines or surfaces; but this conceptual furniture is made to fit the data of experience as closely as possible. In all these cases recourse is made to conceptions more amenable to the operations of thought than are the relatively ragged data provided by experimental results. Ayer makes the mistake of supposing that these abstractions are perfectly arbitrary, that because we form them freely, we must form them entirely at random.

It is, then, unnecessary to suppose that all mathematical propositions differ in any fundamental way from other scientific propositions.[10] There is a theorem, quoted somewhere by Herbert Spencer, of which he says that it never ceased to be a source of wonderment to him, namely that the common tangents of any three circles in a plane meet in the same straight line. This can be deduced from the assumed properties of circles and straight lines.[11] Let us compare this with the proposition from chemistry that a mixture of hydrogen and chlorine exposed to sunlight reacts with explosive violence, which can be shown to be a consequence of the nature of the chlorine and hydrogen molecules. So long as the gases in question were imperfectly known, and chemical knowledge in general was still rudimentary, such phenomena, though they could be observed and registered, could not be deduced from others. It is when we can derive particular instances from principles of wider application that we begin to feel that we know with peculiar certainty. When we recognize a connection between events that at first seemed quite independent, and are able to piece together into some kind of general system a number of happenings that before were isolated and unrelated, then we have the feeling of a necessary sequence, of a solidarity among natural phenomena. It is in the simplest abstract phenomena where only motion, form, and mass are involved that we first reach this stage, and it is therefore first in geometry and mechanics that *a priori* reasoning occurs, the deduction of particular cases from a known general principle. Our feeling of confidence is in proportion to the generality of the principle involved. The chemist's powers of deduction in his own field are, as yet, much inferior to those of the physicist or the mathematician, but they are not different in kind.

There are some things which appear to be inseparable: wherever we find the one we can confidently expect the other. Others are often found together, but sometimes not. Applying an anthropomorphic interpretation, we say of the first pair that they cannot help accompanying or following one another, but of the second that they may occur apart; that in the second case there is a degree of liberty, in the first none. The scientific view of the matter is rather different. If two phenomena are found to be inseparable, then they are independent of all unknown conditions. If the stone always falls to the earth except where it is prevented by some contrary force, then this means that the phenomenon in question is determined by conditions which, so far as we are concerned, are always present, and is not influenced by conditions of which we have no knowledge. If we are not able to say whether a particular phenomenon will occur or not in certain given circumstances, it is because these circumstances are not alone sufficient to determine it: there are others of which we are unaware, or which we cannot calculate, on which it also depends.

There is a memorable experiment described by Köhler.[12] His chimpanzees were accustomed to reach their basket of fruit by swinging on a rope slung on a hook in a beam in the roof. On one occasion he left the rope wound round the beam. Here is a practical situation not easily solved by trial and error because it requires a rather long sequence of co-ordinated movements. Yet there is only one necessary manipulation—that of lifting the loose end and allowing it to fall on the other

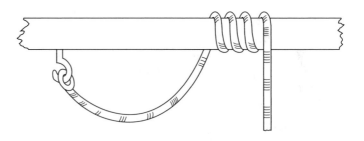

side of the beam. In terms of mechanics we should say that the operation depends on the principle of the coil or loop. If the simple action has been grasped, the repetition can be pictured in the imagination, and the whole sequence can then be 'deduced' from the simple component.

This task is, then, a problem in analysis—of reducing the solution of a situation to a sequence of elementary and familiar acts. As it turned out, the solution was just within the powers of the most intelligent of the apes, although on the first occasion none of the animals succeeded. They tugged at the loose end or fumbled with the loops, and one even removed the rope from the hook. If any of the loops became unwound it was by dint of blind fumbling on the middle ones. The apes were, initially, unable to see what every human sees quite clearly, the essential structure of the situation. However, on a later occasion one of them solved the problem with apparent ease. That was after an interval of two years, but with no further experience of the situation in the meantime. It was naturally difficult for the animals to realize that, in order to bring the loose end finally nearer, they needed initially to throw it further away from themselves.

It is easy enough to complicate such situations beyond the limit of any individual's capacity. There exist all kinds of 'puzzles' involving the same principle of the loop, complicated by different degrees of flexibility of the string or wire or by the number of separate pieces involved. Some people can quickly 'see the way of it', others fumble, but once the trick has been learned, the 'necessity' of the effective manipulation is seen. The more clearly the structure of the puzzle is comprehended, the more inevitable the whole process appears, and such knowledge, although it may have taken time to acquire, seems indubitable. We are not less certain that a rope may be lengthened by uncoiling, or a tangled thread extended into linearity by a finite number of untwistings or unloopings, than we are that an equilateral triangle has equal angles. Indeed, convictions about geometry are derived from experience of physical objects, not *vice versa.* Mathematicians may feel more certitude about their laboriously established equivalences, but the carpenter will rely more confidently on the constant behaviour of his materials. The source of this feeling is a psychological question, as was clearly understood and stated by J.S. Mill.[13]

'Knowledge' is an internal variable state which can be modified by external conditions and which, in turn, determines in part the reactions of the animal. If we take it to mean simply the capacity to act effectively in a particular situation, we may say that some kinds of knowledge do not require to be obtained by experience, for they are inherited. Some animals depend very largely on such knowledge, which we call 'instinct'. Other kinds of animal depend so largely on experience that it is hard to recognize in them any purely instinctive behaviour. In the case of man, who depends more than any other animal on acquired habits, purely reflex acts are relatively few. Nevertheless, we know how to breathe as soon as we are born, and we know the effects of gravitation on our body as soon as we are able to crawl. At a very early age, we know how to put a finger on any visible part of our body or of any neighbouring body. Our nervous system is so organized that these things come naturally to us. But the biologist says that this organization has been slowly acquired in the course of evolution and formed in adaptation to the facts of the world, and that what we do not have to learn in our own lifetime has been gradually learned by our ancestors. If there are 'necessary propositions' which seem to us beyond all possible doubt, it is because our evolutionary development has been constantly guided by the surrounding conditions, and some relations are so familiar to us that we cannot imagine ourselves not knowing them. Le Dantec explains our confidence in the truth of simple arithmetical propositions on this basis.[14] In the same context, he shows that it is not quite impossible to doubt the universal validity of the fundamental operations of arithmetic; for it is (or was) locally believed of a stone in Brittany marked with a number of crosses that they are not to be counted, and that anyone who tries always gets a different result at each attempt. In other words, the total is not independent of the order in which the items are counted. This unusual condition is ascribed to some magical virtue in the stone; but the belief indicates that it is possible to doubt an 'indubitable' proposition of arithmetic. Those propositions called *a priori* or analytic, which are generally held to be indubitable, and for that reason essentially distinct from the empirical propositions of science, are in fact merely statements of inveterate experience, so organized and systematized that each portion carries with it the accumulated conviction earned by the whole. In this way one might claim to have explained the illusion of certainty. But it is misleading to call this an illusion. That two and two make four, that one thing cannot be in two places at once, that the angles of an equilateral triangle are equal—

of these things we are certain in the only intelligible sense of the word. We have no conception of any superior certainty, and this conviction is but the limit of increasing assurance.

Although it is usually elementary propositions of arithmetic or geometry that are cited as examples of 'necessary' truths, the doctrine that there are such truths owes some of its prominence in the history of philosophy to political and religious motives. Leibniz, for instance, in the preface to his *Nouveaux Essais sur l'Entendement* (published only in 1765, nearly 50 years after his death), introduces the topic of necessary truths by mentioning "such as are found in pure mathematics", but is careful to add that ethics, theology, and jurisprudence are "full of such truths". These were much more important for the philosophers of his day than the truths of arithmetic and geometry, although much less easy to illustrate. The mathematical ones are the ones usually mentioned because they are so much more readily accepted.

IV. Sensation and Perception: Ayer and Russell

The normal view of reality—the view which forms the foundation of all daily thoughts and activities—is that there exist all sorts of things of which we know nothing at all, but which we may perhaps come to know in time; that our conception of a thing is quite distinct from the thing itself and may be more or less erroneous. By 'experience' is meant the getting to know things better, observing them, experimenting with them, and so accumulating knowledge about the world; and we are able to investigate the way in which animals, including ourselves, perceive the various things in their environment and form ideas of them in their brains.

Against this normal view of things, sceptics have pointed out that, as our knowledge of the world is restricted to the ideas we form from what we experience through our senses, we cannot be sure that the world we know bears some resemblance or relation to the real world, because we can never compare the two. We have no access to a real world independently of our sensations. It is—so this argument goes—all very well to say that there is a real world which causes these sensations, but even this is merely a dogmatic and groundless assertion, since we have no means of ascertaining the existence of anything beyond our sensations.

Now to say that our sensations are the sole reality makes nonsense of everything. It results in solipsism, the view that I, or my sensations, are the only real thing in the universe; that the Sun, Moon, and stars are but my sensations of them, and that China, Japan, and Australia have no existence apart from the vague conceptions of them existing in my mind. Since someone who really believed this would be mad, philosophers have to find a way out. Accordingly, Ayer seeks a way of reconciling the sceptical view with the normal attitude to reality (p. 130). He does not wish to deny the existence of the real world, yet he wants to retain the doctrine that all our knowledge is made up of sense-data. He supposes that it must be possible to find some form of words in which the external concrete environment can be described without any implications about externality, about reality as distinct from sensory experience—yet without actually denying that there is a reality distinct from sensations. Hence he says that "it is the philosopher's business to give a correct definition of material things in terms of sensations" (pp. 50–51).

This, however, is a hopeless undertaking, as there is no meaning in 'sensations' apart from assumed objects of sense. A sentient being is an animal having eyes, ears, or nose, by which it is made aware of objects and events in its environment; and it is perverse to accept the existence of noses while questioning that of what stimulates them. Delusion and error imply a discrepancy between internal experiences and external events, and have no meaning if applied to either of these without the other. Hence, unless the distinction between real things and our perceptions of them is accepted, there is no longer any meaning in speaking of the senses and sensations.[15]

If I look out of my window, my sensations include an area of green and, at various points, patches of yellow. If I say that I am looking at my lawn and at the daffodils bordering it, I will enable others to picture the scene better. In the one case I describe my sensations, and it is difficult to do so exhaustively, while in the other I describe my perceptions—my interpretation of my sensations—and this is easy. If I go into the garden, I shall still perceive the grass and the flowers, but my sensations will change at every step—another reason why it is vain to attempt to define material things in terms of sensations. Ayer later conceded as much, saying: "You can't reduce even ordinary simple statements about cigarette cases and glasses and ash trays to statements about sense data".[16]

I *experience* my sensations, but I *perceive* the facts to which they testify. Perception depends on pre-existing experiences, and if such earlier experience is insufficient, I may interpret my sensations wrongly. An entomologist sees a butterfly flutter past. He has only seen, for the space of a second, a zig-zagging speck of colour against a background of sky and trees, and has supplied the rest from his expert knowledge. A layman watching the same phenomenon might not know whether he has seen a butterfly or a falling leaf. Perception is therefore an elementary form of reasoning, and reasoning depends on experience and on the power of reviewing experiences and combining and recombining them in the imagination.

The momentary aspect of an object is often a matter of very little importance so long as the inference to the real object is reliable. I know that the post has come, because I heard the postman's knock and the sound of the letter-box. From two brief and indescribable sounds—indescribable, that is, except in terms of such familiar things as knockers and letter-boxes—I infer with perfect confidence that the postman has been, and if I could not act on such inferences throughout every day, life would not be possible. Every animal does the same. Yet what is the postman, and how complex an event is his call at the house! What a vast difference between the brief aspect which it presents to me and the aspect which it presents to the postman himself! Yet if he has occasion to remember or report that he left a letter at my house, and if I have occasion to confirm his statements, we shall both believe that we are referring to one and the same event, and the unity of the event will not be impaired even if no element in his experience of it coincided with any element in mine. Inferences from the sensations to the realities have become so habitual and, in a familiar environment, so reliable, as to disguise how little we can know without the aid of inferences of some kind and to suggest to us that our perceptions are immediate and inference-free.

In sum, it would not be possible, even if it could conceivably be of any use, to abandon altogether the idea of things and describe our experiences as a stream of disconnected sense-data. The terms on which we should have to rely for such a description have been adapted to the hypothesis of a real objective world of which our sense-experiences are merely aspects. The things and events to which we attribute our experiences may be conceived in different ways, and there is no reason why we should not revise our analysis of the world. But if we are to communicate with each other, we must do so in terms of the supposed realities, for we do not and cannot experience the same sensations as one another at the same time.

When Ogden and Richards speak of the "reference" (by which they mean the thought, the idea) "grasping" its object "in greater or less degree", [17] what they have in mind is that the idea of an object consists of memories of a large number of aspects of it. If an observer has never seen a cow except in one particular attitude, in one particular environment, and against one particular background, then his idea of a cow will be inadequate: his 'reference' will not 'grasp' its object. But if he has lived with cows, milked, fed, and tended them, watched them grazing, suckling their calves, and performing all the natural functions of bovine existence, then his reference will have a better grasp of its object. If ten men sit round a recumbent cow, each will contemplate an appreciably different aspect. By exchanging positions they can exchange aspects, and the practical possibility of this simple manoeuvre is the basis of the hypothesis that ascribes all these aspects to a single object. If they are not allowed to change places but may make sketches, they will be able, by passing these round, to elaborate their notion of the animal. The practical experience that all these aspects and many others are equally accessible to each observer, if only he takes the trouble to shift his viewpoint, and that such aspects may be recovered again and again by returning to the appropriate position, gives rise to the notion of a cow as something far more complex than, and including, all these different aspects. Long experience of such animals has probably supplied each of these observers with memories which serve the same purpose as the sketches of his colleagues, so he can recall all the more interesting aspects at will, and the occurrence of any particular one is able to evoke memories of any or all of the others. This bundle of memories taken as a whole—though they can, of course, be recalled only in succession, except insofar as they may become fused and combined —constitutes his 'idea' of this cow as an object; and when he speaks or thinks about it, it is components of this bundle of aspects which recur in his mind. How complete and adequate his idea is will depend on his experience and on his memory; and on the adequacy of his idea will depend the effectiveness of his dealings with the animal. The word 'perception' has long been used in psychology for the process by which the current sensations are compounded with associated memories in the brain to represent things as opposed to their transient aspects.[18]

All this may seem perfectly obvious, but it is often unappreciated, and philosophers write as though a mere aspect constituted an idea. Bertrand Russell, for instance, anxious to undermine our confidence in our everyday beliefs, writes, of chairs, tables, and trees:

> Naive common sense supposes that they are what they appear to be, but that is impossible, since they do not appear exactly alike to any two simultaneous observers. . . . If we are going to admit that the object is not what we see, we can no longer feel the same assurance that there is an object; this is the first intrusion of doubt. (1927, pp. 3–4)

So because the table presents different aspects to you and me who are sitting on opposite sides of it, we must feel some doubt as to whether there really is a table at all! It is, of course, the whole collection of aspects known to us, and their relations to one another and to our actions, which constitutes our idea of the object, and this idea is reckoned to be a true one if in dealing with the object we always find that the aspects succeed one another according to expectation. When a mammal knows how to deal with a particular object, he knows what movements to make to get into a particular relation to it, in other words: to get a particular complex impression from it. It is this knowledge of how the aspects of an object are linked to his own actions which enables him to cope with his environment.

The distinction between a solid object and its

projection on the retina is continually exploited by philosophers to suggest the deceptive nature of commonsense judgements. "We perceive tables as circular", says Russell, "in spite of the fact that a painter, to reproduce their appearance, has to paint ellipses" (1948, p. 21). In fact, however, what is called a circular table is one which gives a circular section perpendicular to a particular axis. To say that any three-dimensional object is circular is untrue if more than this is implied.

How little Russell appreciates the significance of aspect is revealed when he says:

> 'Peter' really covers a number of different occurrences, and is in a sense general. Peter may be near or far, walking or standing or sitting, laughing or frowning. All these produce different stimuli, but the stimuli *have enough in common* to produce the reaction consisting of the word 'Peter'. (1927, p. 56, italics added)

But there is by no means anything common to all the stimuli which evoke the idea of Peter—his voice, his walk, his dress, his handwriting. The idea of Peter may include all this and much more besides, and cannot be dealt with as just the common nucleus of a number of similar experiences. There is no resemblance between a man's voice and his boots, yet even his dog will be able to recognize the common relevance of these two entirely different things.

Russell asks how it is that we can think of a man "as a single quasi-permanent entity" when we see him at one time full-face, at another in profile, and at another from behind. He thinks that it is his "name"—Mr. A.—which makes this "much easier than it would otherwise be" (1948, p. 76). And "whether there is anything identical,

and if so what, between two different appearances
of Mr. A is a dark and difficult question" (p. 81).
But it is quite unnecessary for there to be any
'identity' between the front and back views of the
gentleman for even a dog—ignorant of his name
—to be able to recognize him from both aspects.
Russell supposes that "words and ideas are in
fact, interchangeable" (p. 111). It would be truer
to say that the idea of a situation is adequate in
proportion as it initiates behaviour appropriate to
the situation, and that the verbal description of a
situation is adequate in proportion as it generates
such an idea in the mind of him who hears it.
Russell seems so often to write about something
before he has thought much about it.[19] If only
philosophers would inquire how animals form
their ideas of things, how their miscellaneous
experiences get integrated into notions of permanent objects, how these ideas are awakened by
sensations, and how the behaviour of the animal
is influenced by his ideas! A friend of mine was
struck by the behaviour of a Siamese cat of his
acquaintance who took a great interest in the
television when there were birds on the screen.
She even went behind the set and clawed at the
casing, obviously thinking that the birds she
could see on the screen were inside the set, and
could be caught if only she could penetrate it. But
one does not have to rely on such unusual
evidence to realize that a cat can recognize a real
bird or mouse from any presented aspect of sight
or sound or, in the case of the mouse, from its
smell. That Russell makes quite inadequate al-
lowance for animals' knowledge is clear from his
statement that "without the corroboration of testimony we should hardly have had much confidence in the existence of physical objects. . . . It

is the similarity between the perceptions of different people in similar situations that makes us feel
confident of the external causation of our perceptions; but for this, whatever naïve beliefs we
might have had in physical objects would have
been dissipated long ago" (1927, p. 6). So that
cats and dogs, who are not in a position to seek
the "corroboration of testimony", cannot be supposed to have "much confidence in the existence
of physical objects".

The ideas of things which underlie such
behaviour of course vary enormously in complexity as between different kinds of animal. The
bookcase, if it is for the dog a thing at all, is just a
bulky object where his ball or his bone may be
concealed, and from under which these may be
extracted by certain muscular exertions. The
bookcase is defined by what he can do about it, or
what it can do to him. To a dog, a chair is as much
a part of the house's immovable fixtures as is a
bookcase. He will jump on to it if it affords him a
route to something he wants, but to move it to a
more favourable position for such use is beyond
his capacity, although well within that of a chimpanzee, whose idea of the thing is correspond-
ingly more complex. Lowly animals lack any
capacity to integrate aspects into an idea of an
object, and so cannot respond to an object unless
it is presented to them in the one particular
aspect which they can recognize. Display behaviour obviously has the function, among others, of
presenting a particular and easily recognizable
aspect to another animal. Many animals that do
not have the complex brains which facilitate
recognition of an object from any presented
aspect rely more on sound and smell than on
sight, for these do not vary in the same way as do

visual data according to the point from which they are perceived, but only as to the strength or weakness of the signal.

One reason why so many writers fail to appreciate the complexity of human ideas is that we seem to be able to use them as if they were instantaneous. This they cannot be, but they are of much shorter duration than the experiences and exploratory movements which go to form them, and we are able to conceive in a moment many of the complex relations of an object or situation which we could describe only at considerable length. When we think of a situation, we are often able to see what we must do about it, or what is to be expected of it, and to act accordingly: a concept which includes or consists of a very large store of information on a subject can be mobilized very quickly. This is very noticeable in the case of trained scientists. When the inexpert thinks, for instance, of an elephant, what passes through his mind may be no more than some faint memory from a picture-book; and as he does not have to reason about elephants—he need not consider, for example, whether they in any way resemble fish—this frailty of conception is not felt as a hindrance. But the zoologist is able after the briefest reflection to answer all kinds of question about the elephant which seem to involve years of study and experience. The idea which can be built up only by prolonged and arduous study seems, when it is completed, to be reduced to a curt formula or condensed picture which in some way adequately represents the whole system of information from which it is derived.

Any explanation of this must surely include some reference to the fact that a particular problem, when it arises, has the power of reviving those memories that are relevant. For instance, I wish to have a rose. I know that I must go downstairs and through the back door into the garden before I can get into the necessary relation with the rosebush, and that I must collect a knife from the kitchen on the way. But I do not have to picture the process of opening the door of my room, crossing the landing, descending the stairs, and so forth, for all these actions are familiar and I know that they are easily accomplished. There need be little on my mind except the idea of the goal. Thus, to the question: what is the idea in the mind that is effective, we can answer: it is often the idea of a result, together with a feeling of confidence that it can be achieved by initiating a certain course of activity.

Suppose now that I wish to put a box, not at present visible, into a cupboard I am inspecting. To see whether the space suffices, I have to call the box to mind, but I have no need to think of its colour or contents. Then I think of lifting it up to stow it away, and this recalls its great weight and perhaps also its lack of handles. Thus each particular character of the object remains in abeyance, a merely potential memory, until the situation envisaged requires it. When we make use of some complex object, for example as a tool, we generally do so in virtue of some particular property it possesses. On different occasions we may use the same object for different purposes, and so exploit different qualities, but what we call the object's qualities are the ways in which it can be used. As our needs and methods grow more complicated, we recognize ever more qualities in things. Since it often happens that many quite different things can be used for one and the same purpose, we say that they have a quality in common, and in our thoughts we separate this quality, as an abstraction, and work out our plans in terms of it, without burdening our minds with all the miscellaneous and variable concomitants which accompany it in the real world. Sharpness, for instance, is that quality which makes a tool useful for cutting, and when we reckon with the possibility of separating a solid piece of matter into parts, we do not have to review a whole range of tools—knife, chisel, axe, or razor—but need think only of the cutting process or of its effects.

Hence, if an idea is too scanty, it will be unreliable, but if it is too full, it will be cumbersome and slow in action. The very rapidity of thought processes shows that some greatly abridged substitute for a complete idea must replace it for most purposes.

There is no reason why the brief mental representative constituting an abstraction need be a word, but it frequently is: the word 'sharp' is associated with all the different concrete experiences which underlie the abstraction and is able under favourable circumstances to recall them. But as what is actually in the mind at a given moment may be no more than the word, it is easy to suppose that the idea involves nothing else, or that, as Russell holds, "words and ideas are interchangeable". In truth, however, this is the case only with practical affairs that are very familiar to us: within this compass, reliance on verbalized mental processes is continually justified, as Englefield illustrates:

> From the bare statement in the news bulletin that it is going to rain, we may decide on an appropriate course of action without any mental representation of streaming windows

or puddles and mud. From the verbal announcement of a particular event we may jump directly to the verbal statement of the probable consequence without the mediation of any concrete imagery. But this sort of verbal reasoning can only be valid where the linkage is familiar and habitual . . . It is . . . only in the realm of customary events and well established correlations among familiar things that inferences from verbal formulas, unsupported by any reference, either external or imaginative, to concrete realities are not precarious.[20]

The problems about appearance and reality that have made so many philosophers fight shy of committing themselves to a clear distinction between a real world and ideas of that world arise only when we begin to think about our own ideas, rather than of those of other persons or of animals;[21] for we form our conceptions of the outside world and of the contrast between it and the inside world, by observing these others. When I observe my neighbour, I see him immersed in an environment external to him and perfectly distinct from him. From his actions and his words I gather that he possesses some kind of internal apparatus which, more or less imperfectly, represents for him the environment. Parts of his environment which I can observe, but which are not for the moment observable by him, nevertheless appear to play as definite a part in determining his behaviour as those parts which he can observe. This leads me to suppose that he possesses an internal representation of the environment which can supplement and complete the more or less fragmentary aspects of it which are presented to him at any moment.[22] Since he makes mistakes, that is acts sometimes as if his environment were other than it is, I get from observing him the idea of error and illusion. If there were no other human beings or animals in the world, or if I were perpetually secluded from them, I should perhaps have some difficulty in reaching these notions, as my own illusions are apt to seem real to me.

Besides my fellow mortals, my experience includes my own body, and I am able to recognize a number of common characters in their bodies and my own which lead me to a comparison and to a transfer of properties. Although I have never seen my own back, I find it convenient to assume that I have a back like theirs. Because I have grown up in society and learned a language where parts of the body are named, such comparison was suggested to me and made much easier than it might otherwise have been. I have, however, other means of knowing my own body which I miss in the case of others. I can know its position in the dark; I can 'feel' my own limbs, that is know their position and attitude by means of a sense which is distinct from sight, hearing, or touch—a sense by means of which I know nothing at all about other people.

In sum, with some of my senses I can make a more complete study of my neighbour than I can of myself. With others I am better placed in regard to my own body. The result is that when I come to compare his body and his behaviour with my own, I find it helpful to supplement both my idea of him and my idea of myself by borrowing from one or the other in turn. My visual exploration of him supplements my incomplete visual knowledge of myself: and my private knowledge of myself supplements my ideas of him, as when I assume that he has feelings like mine—an assumption that enables me more readily to account for his behaviour and to anticipate it.

Now in accordance with this general principle of supplementing my knowledge of myself from observations of others, and *vice versa,* I find myself trying to contrast my own ideas with the things they represent. But there the difficulty begins, for I can make no such comparison. What were for me the real things when I was considering my neighbour and his ideas of them are no longer anything but ideas when I transfer the inquiry to myself. All the useful relationships which I had established between his mind and the features of his external environment cease to be applicable in my own case. To any individual the whole world is accessible only in the representative form which it assumes in his own brain. He can obviously not escape from that position, and if he wants to speculate about the world, he must speculate about the world which is accessible to him. So far as he is concerned, there is no world that is more real than that. In order to understand the reflections and actions of his neighbour, he has to take some real world for granted, just as when one wants to measure a velocity, one must take some co-ordinate system at rest for granted. The fact that no absolute co-ordinate system can be determined is no serious inconvenience. But idea and reality, which are both accessible to him when he is studying his neighbour's ideas and environment, are not contrastable in the same way when he is studying his own ideas of the world. In other words, if John and Henry wish to discuss the adequacy of certain ideas as representations of certain objects, they must avoid any attempt to compare their own ideas with reality. John's own ideas may be consistent, and that, for him, is an important criterion of their truth. But Henry's ideas (as known to John) may be compared directly by John with reality (as it appears to John). Likewise, John's ideas (as known to Henry) may be compared directly by Henry with the reality (as it appears to Henry). But John's own ideas (as known to himself) cannot be compared with any independent reality by John, to whom reality is known only from his ideas. The two sets of data—the one set concerning one's neighbour and the other set oneself—cannot be completely superposed.

In normal life, then, we judge the truth of someone's ideas by comparing them with the facts, but the problem is: how can we judge the truth of our own ideas, since all the facts are known to us only in the form of our own ideas? It is no solution to say that ideas constitute the sole reality: that would merely illustrate how easy it is to reason with words; for what is an idea? Unless we can contrast it with the reality, and distinguish between real things or events and the notion which someone has about them; unless we can distinguish someone's bodily form and visible behaviour from those internal and invisible processes we call his thoughts or ideas, we cannot say what we mean by an idea, nor what we mean by reality. In that case, there would not be much advantage in saying that the one is the same as the other. The solution is possible only if we allow that, when we speak or think of 'ideas', we are employing a notion which we owe in part to our ideas and our reflections on them, and in part to the supposed ideas of other persons to which we attribute their behaviour. Where another person's ideas are concerned, we can often see the facts more readily than he, and can see not only that he is mistaken, but also why. Where our own ideas are concerned we cannot assume this objective standpoint. We can only act on our idea and see whether the result is in accordance with expectation.

I will try to summarize. Common sense distinguishes the concrete things of our environment from the ideas of them which we have in our minds. But some metaphysicians have said: Stuff and nonsense! The things are nothing but your ideas of them. What do you know of the things save what gets somehow into your mind? You do not know the things at all, you know but the picture gallery in your own consciousness which you say—quite unjustifiably—represents them. To such a metaphysician who supposes it possible to hold that there is no reality apart from what is in his mind, the reply must be made that an inside presupposes an outside, that someone's whole conception of ideas inside a mind and an environment outside it is derived from his experience of other persons and of animals; and that if we discard the teaching of experience, we must discard also the distinction between outside and inside.

V. The Religious Reaction: Ward

The inadequacy of views such as those of Russell and Ayer outlined above has occasioned a strong religious reaction. Professor Keith Ward, now Regius Professor of Divinity at Oxford, tells that he turned to Christianity from dissatisfaction with philosophers concerned to demolish even commonsense convictions—in particular "positivists" who, he says, "analysed things like tables into sets of purely private sense-data which were not enduring material objects at all". Such philosophers "went out of their way to deny that they could tell us any truths about the world", and were content with "just analysing the meanings of words". One can sympathize with his desire for an outlook that comes to grips with "the way things are, including issues such as abortion, euthanasia and nuclear deterrence".[23]

Reasoning involves inhibition from action while thinking out the best way of dealing with a situation. It is thus essentially a delaying process, and, if prolonged, can undermine the will to action. This, says Ward, was his own pre-Christian situation: he "had the endemic disease of all intellectuals, being paralysed by an excess of rationality". He now favours "the religious vision" because it is not only a way of seeing the world, but also "commitment to a course of action within it"—a commitment namely to love, "spelt out by reference to the vision of God seen in the person of Jesus Christ" (pp. 74–75).

Ward's reaction takes the form of supposing that much knowledge can be had directly, without any process of inference from other data. He mentions "the old philosophical puzzle" of how we can know that people other than ourselves have ideas and emotions; for we have direct access only to our own minds. It would, one might add, be easy for an engineer to design a machine that squeals whenever it is kicked, and no one would suppose that such a machine thinks or feels anything. It is presumably with such considerations in mind that Ward asks why it is that we rightly reject the possibility that other people are likewise "just responding to stimuli, without any real feelings". He declines the obvious answer, namely that their whole behaviour suggests to us the presence of the kind of mental apparatus that we know underlies our own activity. The truth is that we cannot make sense of the behaviour even of other mammals without such a theory. When bananas lie out of reach outside the bars of a chimpanzee's cage, he will go and fetch a stick and drag them in with it. He does not do something totally inappropriate such as standing on his head or climbing on boxes. One can account for what he actually does only by assuming that he has some mental representation both of the actual situation and also of how to convert it into the more desirable one. In general terms, an animal's experimental behaviour is not quite random, but is usually relevant to the instinct which initiates it. If an animal wants food, he acts in what appears to be a sensible way, a way that is likely to bring him into contact with the kind of food he needs. It is the lack of any simple correspondence between the stimulus of the situation on the animal's sensorium and his response to it that compels us to posit an intervening process in his mind. Ward, however, maintains that "we do not have to infer that our parents and children have feelings; we jolly well know that they do. . . . It is a given datum of experience". And he "suggest[s] that something the same is true of faith in God"; for "people do not believe or disbelieve in God because they have gone through some set of arguments or assembled the right sort of evidence" (pp. 71–72).

I agree that many believe in God not because

of a conscious decision taken after weighing evidence; but this is very often because their minds are closed to all criticism, which they deem not even worthy of consideration. Ward's idea seems to be that we can have immediate knowledge of God because he, like the people we know, is a person, although more of a spirit than they: "We no more need to prove the existence of God than we need to prove the existence of our friends. Given the fundamental belief that reality expresses Spirit, what we need to know is, where it is best, most fully expressed" (1982, p. 6). Nonetheless, he allows that belief in God is a datum of experience only "for those who have it", and he realizes that this is rather an important qualification; for while everyone believes in other people and their feelings, not everyone believes in God. He even concedes that "there are very good reasons for not believing in God", and that "the existence of vast and terrible suffering counts against the existence of a loving God". Hence "belief in God is an option", and we must "choose the basic options by which we live" (p. 72). But he has clearly convinced himself that his own choice is no arbitrary one.

Ward writes as he does because he does not accept that *every* interpretation of perceptual data is a hypothesis, whether what is involved is supplying in our minds the missing part of a supposed sequence or the unperceived aspects of a thing. It is, for example, a hypothesis that the series of visual experiences which I have from day to day when I turn my eyes toward the sky can be attributed to a constant body, the sun, which reappears periodically, and not to a procession of similar bodies, as was supposed by Xenophanes in the sixth century B.C.[24] Again, when I see the familiar face of the postman each morning, it is a hypothesis that these intermittent experiences are due to the continued existence of a being which only at intervals comes into my sight. We think of things as continuous, yet the evidence we have is interrupted and desultory. In many cases we make the relevant assumptions with such confidence that we are not conscious of making any hypothesis, but viewed as a mental process it is the same, regardless of the degree of certainty we may feel. In sum, understanding someone's behaviour (including the words he speaks) involves an inference from something observed to something not observed, and is therefore a particular case of a wider class of mental processes. Even the conception of a concrete object involves an inference from the particular aspect observed to the object as a whole.

The choice between fact and fantasy which we make when deciding on what to believe is fundamentally the same choice which we often make between true memories and mere figments of imagination. I am now in my study, but I have mental images of myself being in town earlier in the day. Whether I class these as memory or imagination depends on my construction of the world, or of my own part of it. If these images fit into this construction, I accept them as memories, otherwise not. Immediately past events are so closely related to the present situation that it is fairly easy to fit them on to it and so to recognize their mental representation as memory. Remoter events cannot be classified so easily, but some kinds of fantasy can be recognized at once as not directly derived from experience because we regard the events they allege as impossible. If I seem to remember floating out of the window, I do not accept this as a true memory because it is not conformable to my idea of how the world is organized. In cases where the alleged memory is not of an event in itself impossible, I must take into consideration other memories and present conditions, and inquire whether the rest of the world, as now presented to me, is compatible with this being a memory. If not, I must either suppose myself to be deluded now, or else to be dealing not with a memory but with a fantasy.

There is no difference at all in the mental image itself, whether it derives from an experience directly, in other words is a memory, or is a recombination of elements of experience. The difference between memory and imagination, therefore, is not so much one of feeling as of judgment. Most so-called memories contain a fair admixture of imagination, and the most fantastic chimera which we may conceive is derived from elements of experience. There is, then, no clear line of division between memory and imagination. When, for instance, one recalls experiences, there are gaps in one's memories, to be filled with conjectures; and when these memories are later again recalled, the conjectured experiences which filled gaps in the first recall are themselves as much part of the recall as the original experiences; so that one may easily take for fact what originated as conjecture linking facts. There are endless opportunities here for error.

Alexander Bain implies that there is a specific feeling that distinguishes a true memory from something merely imagined. He says: "I believe that I yesterday ran up against a wall to keep out of the way of a carriage"; and he adds: "I feel that if there were any likelihood of being jammed up in that spot again, I should not go that way if I could help it."[25] But surely he might resolve to avoid that route merely if he had read in the newspaper of an accident of the same kind which had occurred to someone else. His desire to avoid that narrow lane is evidence of the belief that it is dangerous, not that he encountered a carriage with a reckless driver there. If he had to prove that he had been there, he would do so by recalling many subsequent experiences which were related to the incident—what he said to his wife on reaching home, the plaster still on his grazed fingers, his muddied trousers still hanging up in the kitchen to dry—in fact the present situation in the home would be in many respects different from what it in fact is if the incident had never really happened. Belief in past experiences can be confirmed only by the unique compatibility of those experiences with the present observable situation. If the belief is well founded, then this or that result must now be discoverable. If we then say that belief rests on coherence with other memories and experiences, we must allow that such coherence is estimated differently by different animals or men, and that, as behaviour grows more complicated and depends on a greater number of circumstances, the power of estimating coherence must be increased, and the likelihood of error and illusion also.

One thing that distinguishes the memories we have of dreams from memories of waking experiences is that, in dreams, there is no going back to have a second look at a situation. If Bain had returned to the scene of the occurrence with the carriage, he might have found the marks of the carriage wheels and traces of his own footprints in the mud. If in a dream I observe some striking object, I may investigate it, and it often proves to be something entirely different from what I thought, and indeed may change into something else even while I am attending to it. I cannot possibly get back to my original position to start the examination all over again and check my results. An object that we experience when awake, however unusual its shape, presents a sequence of aspects as we move our position in regard to it, but this sequence is linked to the sequence of our movements. I expect, and I invariably find where real experiences are concerned, that all the aspects are compatible and that the transition from one to another is nowhere arbitrary. I am not saying that all our experience of the real world is free from inconsistencies and inconsequences, only that it is these characters by which we recognize the real.

The historian goes to work in the same way as any ordinary individual in deciding between fact and fiction, and his criterion is partly general: such and such things certainly happen, but it does not follow that a particular alleged instance of them happened; to establish that it did, it is necessary to see how it fits in with other events regarded as established. On the other hand, such and such things do not happen, and evidence that they do must be explained in some other way unless it is so strong as to compel abandonment of the premiss that they do not. For a long time a controversy raged in archeological circles about certain broken flints in deposits of Pliocene age. Some held that they had been deliberately chipped by primitive men for use as tools, others that their shape owed nothing to human agency. The question was whether some forerunner of man, capable of rudely fashioning flints into tools, already existed in those times. It seems to be now agreed that flints of the same form can be produced by mere pressure in the ground. But suppose that in these same deposits somebody had found a cigarette-lighter or a pair of nail-scissors. Even if no theory could be found to account for their presence there, they would not have been regarded as tools of Pliocene man, for the re-arrangement of all our views about the history of the earth and of mankind, as well as of our elementary conceptions of chemical change, would be too much to ask for the sake of these isolated documents.

The question of the resurrection of Jesus is simpler, in that, to decide that the relevant stories are legends, we do not need to be dogmatically unwilling to make any exception to our experience that dead men do not rise from their graves, but can point out that the evidence that Jesus did so has been admitted even by many theologians, past and present, to be far from conclusive.[26]

In a book entitled *Divine Action,* published by Collins in 1990, Ward maintains that the reliability of the Bible has been put in question only because it has been approached from sceptical premises which look askance at miracles and are mistrustful of all documents from early civilizations. He holds that, if one comes to it from theistic premises, then it is quite credible; for "what is likely to happen if there is a God is quite different from what is likely to happen if there is not" (p. 237). But a major reason for mistrusting the Bible is not the premises one brings to study of it, but crass incompatibilities between its various accounts of what purport to be the same events (or even within one account of a series of events). Ward accepts the Pentateuch's story of the Exodus from Egypt as historically correct; but

Bishop Colenso long ago showed that its items cannot be made to add up to a credible story. As for the New Testament, what Matthew has to say about the circumstances of Jesus's birth and infancy is quite incompatible with what Luke reports about them. Reports of the circumstances and nature of Jesus's resurrection-appearances differ substantially. What miracles he performed, what doctrines he taught, what he said on the cross—all this depends to a considerable extent on which gospel one consults. Then there is the failure of Christian writers earlier than the gospels to confirm anything like their accounts of him. These are just as much problems for the theist, and do not arise from an unduly sceptical approach to the documents.

Ward takes the view that we hardly ever have decisive testimony concerning anything past: "we can very rarely establish exactly what happened even in the next room an hour ago" (p. 242), and so we must not expect indubitable evidence that God has disclosed himself in history. But it is absurd to suggest that, because I may not be quite sure that my wife was ironing in the house earlier today, I am entitled to accept accounts in ancient documents that are full of contradictions, and where one account, even if not contradicted, is uncorroborated by another concerning events which—if they had really happened—must have been of major concern to the authors of both.

Ward believes not only that the Bible contains a credible record of God's past acts, but also that it records "the promises . . . of his future purposes" (p. 240). But I do not see how we can accept the New Testament promise that the world would end in the lifetime of the early Christians; nor does the prediction of a judgement of hellfire carry much conviction today, even in many theological circles. He stresses that the authors of the New Testament wrote from faith, and faith tells "the story of a personal encounter which evoked one's total commitment". He adds: "The story never becomes non-historical, for it is founded on a historical occasion of discernment" —as if what is discerned is never wrong ('non-historical') because discerned on a particular (a 'historical') occasion. This is the merest playing with words. He feels obliged to allow that a sacred story, like others, is apt to change and grow with the telling: it possesses "a semiotic dimension, enshrining, preserving and seeking to evoke new levels of meaning which the community discerns in its original narrative". But he will not have any such accretions stripped off: "The semiotic dimension is in principle beyond the reach of the critical historian. He must register its presence while refraining from commenting on its truth" (pp. 238f).

Ward also stresses that evidence which might fail to convince an isolated inquirer looks more impressive "in the context of participation in a worshipping community." "Experiential participation in the living church" and "community of faith" can make all the difference (p. 239). This merely means that it is easy to believe what one's chosen fellows appear to believe, and is true of communities of Marxists, Fascists, Hindus, and atheists, without making any of their beliefs better founded. And they too might be sufficiently ill-advised to claim a "semiotic dimension" to their articles of faith.

Finally, Ward expresses an emphasis on "spirit" which, as we shall see, informs his whole outlook:

For Christians the life of Jesus is seen as the supreme and definitive case of the sacramental character of the material world, wherein a perfected human nature openly manifests the infinite spiritual reality which is its true basis and goal. (pp. 243–44)

In the early stages of the centuries-long debate about matter and spirit, the two were not fundamentally opposed: spirit was something which had some of the properties of matter, but not others, being, for instance, frequently visible but not tangible. Justification for such selectiveness was found in the experience that prominent properties of matter are not present in all matter: gases and vapours were without shape, were often invisible, and seemed also to be non-resistant and without weight. However, as methods of measurement improved, it became possible to detect the weight of air (Pascal, Torricelli), and the use of air pumps showed that air is resistant. Gradually all material properties were withdrawn from the idea of spirit, and the word was sometimes used as a synonym for mind, sometimes for the intellectual (excluding the emotional) processes (Descartes), and sometimes for consciousness. Each generation reads the works of its predecessors and tries to understand them in terms of its own somewhat different ideas. The confusion and complexity increase progressively.

'Spirit' is wanted for its religious value, but must be represented as scientifically valid. This is most safely done by pulverizing theories that do without it. Ward rejoices because "the clockwork universe that Newton constructed, with its solid little atoms bouncing off one another, has now been demolished" (*The Turn of the Tide,* BBC Publications, 1986, p. 45). We are invited to suppose that this leaves 'spirit' in sole possession of the field. If matter consists of minute solid spheres, then it can be expected to behave in certain ways. These expectations were tested and found to be not always fulfilled, so that modifications had to be introduced into the atomic model. But what can one predict on the basis of the hypothesis that matter is fundamentally 'spiritual'?

VI. Reality as 'Spirit': Ward, Teilhard, and Altizer

We saw Ward contending that "reality expresses Spirit". "Spirit", he says, "is the ultimate basis of the world" (1982, p. 8). Some 20 years earlier, J.A.T. Robinson insisted, in his *Honest to God* (London: S.C.M., 1963) that "reality at its deepest level, is personal" (p. 48). Such determination to fix on one substance, or supposed substance, as underlying all others has been a familiar philosophical ploy from presocratic times. For Thales, the ultimate substance was water; for Anaximenes, air. Heraklitus seems to have felt that such accounts of things left out the human soul or vital principle, and so he supposed that all things are transformations of fire, the most subtle of all vapours because it cannot be captured and bottled. One philosopher would explain the phenomena of life by means of a model based on non-living things, while another did the reverse and tried to explain the non-living world in terms of a notion derived from observing men and animals. Early theories of the soul commonly consisted in some kind of material model (the breath, the shadow, the reflection, the echo, or various vaporous forms); but once the conception of the soul is established, it in turn is available to serve as model for the interpretation of non-human phenomena.

The determination to bring everything under a single explanatory principle is seen again in the Pythagorean obsession with number. Bulk and weight can be denoted by number, and the Greeks discovered, further, many relations between shape and number—length, area, and volume to begin with, and then the relative dimensions of parts of geometrical figures. They were also much impressed by the discovery of the regular solids, with their obvious numerical associations. To these were added the relation between number and musical notes. In view of all these observations, it seems natural that certain philosophers should exaggerate the importance of this mathematical aspect of things; and as there are always people who, when they get a new idea, will try to extend its application to everything, we seem to have a plausible explanation for Pythagoreanism.

Such premature generalization is a continuing source of error. If so much can be interpreted in terms of one single principle, is it not reasonable to expect that, when the secrets of all things are revealed, the whole universe will appear interpretable in the same terms? And so we come to present-day interpretations of the whole reality as 'spirit' or 'person'.

It is not surprising that those who regard God as some kind of person have their 'vision' of him—as Ward says of his own theism—in Jesus: for the person of God the Father (and also of the Holy Spirit) has become a little vague, and it is much easier to envisage Jesus as a person. Other religions have also found it convenient to produce a more human deputy for God, and the older gods have in this way been gradually displaced by their more personable children. At one stage, God was pictured as a kind of superman, with immense powers, a human though superior intellect, and human emotions—approving, disapproving, loving, and hating, although on the whole just, at least to those he loves. Ward, however, speaks rather of "the personalness of things at their deepest level of being", of a "presence" in our total environment which is "best described as personal or like that experienced in human interpersonal relationships". Hence, when we speak of God, we are "trying to express something about the character of the universe as a whole", not talking about a particular object within it (pp. 74–75). Yet he has not completely freed himself from older views, for he says that God is not only "in" all finite things, but also "beyond them all, as we see them" (1982, p. 9). At times he relapses into quite traditional formulations, as when he speaks of God declaring his purpose through revelation, and of writings which "may reveal his will and purpose", and which "disclose the essential character of the world, its origin and basis in a personal will" (p. 77). When a metaphysician introduces a fresh meaning for a word by means of some arbitrary definition, he is apt to think that it necessarily supersedes the traditional meanings. Yet when he uses the word, it is evident that the thought in his mind is an incoherent complex derived from the older meanings which he has tried somehow to fuse into one.

Ward's talk of 'spirit' as "the ultimate basis of the world" lies firmly in the German metaphysical tradition. Hegel says, in the preface to his *Phänomenologie des Geistes,* that spirit alone is real ("Das Geistige allein ist das Wirkliche"). This tradition has been popularized in Britain by translations of the works of Teilhard de Chardin, a French Jesuit who died in 1955. Medawar, in a very effective and critical review of Teilhard's *The Phenomenon of Man* (1959), quotes him as saying that we are "logically forced to assume the existence in rudimentary form . . . of some sort of psyche in every corpuscle".[27] Because of the popularity of such views, Ward's reaction against 'positivistic' philosophers has fallen on well-prepared ground.

Teilhard was not worried by problems concerning the reliability of the gospels or the correctness of the Church's major theological doctrines. He does not seem to have been aware that awkward questions were being asked on this score, and that it was becoming increasingly difficult to ignore them. What bothered him was that he found the injunction to remain unspotted from the world difficult to reconcile with his passion for digging for fossils. He did not wish to think this activity mere indulgence, and he reconciled the two sides of his life with mystical formulas which imply that even matter is in some sense spiritual. In a letter which he wrote by way of self-justification to the General of his religious order, he speaks of his "profound 'feeling' for the organic realness of the world". At first, he says, "it was an ill-defined feeling in my mind and heart, but as the years have gone by it has gradually become a precise compelling sense of the Universe's general convergence upon itself".[28] He means that, over the years, he has learned to construct phrases about this 'feeling' which sounded to him as if they meant something—as when he adds that this "convergence of the universe upon itself . . . coincides with, and culminates at its zenith in" Jesus—"him *in quo omnia constant";* and that there is a "progression and synthesis of all things in *Xristo Jesu".* Theologians have found such talk to their liking, although they do express reservations. In a symposium entitled *Teilhard Reassessed* (London: Darton, Longman, and Todd, 1970), the editor, Antony Hanson, said of him: "As in the case of Dietrich Bonhoeffer, we do not always know what he meant" (p. vii). That is the great strength of such writers; for what is not understood cannot be refuted.

Hegelian-inspired emphasis on 'spirit' reached the height of incoherence in the so-called 'Death of God' theology in the 1960s. Thomas Altizer then offered what he called "a theological analysis based on the Christian visions of Blake, Hegel, and Nietzsche", and declared that the message the Christian is now called to proclaim is "the glad tidings of the death of God". According to this 'analysis', God did once exist as a purely supernatural spirit, but he then negated himself, emptied himself of such status by becoming completely incarnate in Jesus. When Jesus died, God "passed through what . . . Hegel dialectically conceived as the negation of negation" and did not resume his former transcendence, but moved forward into mankind, where he is again continually 'negated'. "Spirit" is thus continually metamorphosed into "flesh", and is "continually negating or annihilating itself as it ever moves forward to an eschatological goal". Only by so doing can it sustain itself, for Hegel, says Altizer, "maintains that Spirit has real or actual existence only insofar as it alienates itself from itself". God, then, is "a forward-moving process of kenotic metamorphosis who remains himself even while passing through a movement of absolute self-negation". It follows that to believe in Jesus's resurrection and ascension would be to reverse the direction of movement actually taken by God, which was first "forward . . . to Jesus" and thence to "the universal body of humanity, thereby undergoing an epiphany in every human hand and face". It also follows that we "must look upon both the New Testament and early Christianity as exotic and alien forms of religion".[29]

In this type of writing, formulas familiar from the history of philosophy do duty for intelligible propositions, a fanciful, fairy-tale structure passes for a theory, everything that requires verification is merely alleged, and prophetic utterance replaces tentative suggestion. Confronting such apologists makes one feel like trying to lecture on insanity to an audience of lunatics.

ᵉ꘠ 2
Behaviorism and Reaction Against It

I. Watson and Ryle

That thinking is no more than a kind of talking to oneself is the doctrine of J.B. Watson's *Psychology from the Standpoint of a Behaviorist,* 1919. (My quotations are from the third, revised, edition; Philadelphia and London: Lippincott, 1929.) He supposes that thought is "the action of language mechanisms" (p. 347); and where such activity cannot be observed, as when someone is thinking silently, he blames our inadequate methods of observation and claims that nevertheless the "laryngeal, tongue and speech muscles" are active, possibly more active than are the relevant muscles when one is playing tennis (p. 15). When we think of a familiar voice we are, then, presumably imitating it under our breath with our own vocal organs; and if we think of the sound of a violin or a trumpet, or of wind or rain or anything else, we are either just saying the name of the thing to ourselves, without really thinking of it at all, or we reproduce the name laryngeally, albeit silently.

Watson then modifies this view to the extent of allowing that the movements of writing, drawing, and gesticulating may constitute "non-language forms of thought" (p. 355). It would follow that, when we think of a familiar face, we are really performing the movements of drawing it or tracing it with the fingers. In fact, of course, I can recall in a brief instant events and scenes which I could not describe or paint or 'trace with my fingers' even if I had unlimited time for the operation. As Hobbes said, "thought is quick" (*Leviathan*, Chapter 3); but Watson supposes that it is no quicker than our clumsy verbal or manual attempts to express it.

It is probably true that, for many people, abstract thought is possible only as a kind of imagined monologue; for words and sentences are learned with great facility from books or in lecture rooms, whereas ideas of any generality are formed only slowly and with difficulty. Those who observe the predominant role played in their own thought processes by verbal formulas which evoke nothing else except additional verbal formulas may easily come to suppose that the higher kinds of reflection are purely verbal. But it is hard to understand how they can overlook the less abstract mental representations. Can Watson really suppose that our ideas of ordinary everyday things can be analyzed into muscular actions of larynx or finger? If behaviorists have solved no problems in psychology, they have at least enriched the science by presenting it with a new problem—that of themselves.

Watson is understandably embarrassed when he comes to discuss fatigue, which he says is "not a serviceable concept in Psychology"; and in his view most of the relevant literature is best ignored. In particular, he objects to the distinction between 'mental' and 'physical' fatigue as "a most pernicious way of splitting up human activity" (p. 379). Obviously, mental fatigue would imply mental work, which in turn implies the activity of some part of the body other than mere muscle. Its investigation would involve scrutiny of processes which occur in neurones, synapses, and so forth. But as soon as the activities of the brain and central nervous system are taken into account as factors in behaviour, the necessity for explaining thought as laryngeal responses disappears.

Watson, then, has to face two kinds of adversary: the physiologist and the introspective psychologist. The former he can answer only by belittling the importance of the neurobiological processes. The latter he can deal with rather more plausibly by pointing (p. 1) to the obvious abuses resulting from metaphysical speculation. In fact his whole doctrine is based on the conviction that, if psychology is to be of practical use, it must pay more attention to behaviour and less to speculations concerning the states of consciousness. These latter might be argued about indefinitely, and so he thinks it better to base psychology on data that can be observed. Thus he says that, while we cannot at present—because we do not yet have adequate instruments—watch the play of the "implicit stream of words" which for him constitutes silent thinking, "there is no reason for hypothecating a mystery about it. Could we bring 'thinking' out for observation as readily as we can tennis-playing or rowing, the need of 'explaining' it would disappear" (p. 15). But if visible behaviour needs no explanation, and if all behaviour is essentially visible, what are the behaviorist psychologists engaged on? Do we not try to explain the visible behaviour of our neighbours, of animals, of all kinds of inanimate things?

" 'States of consciousness' ", says Watson, "like the so-called phenomena of spiritualism, are not objectively verifiable and for that reason can never become data for science" (p. 2). The comparison is rather strange, since spiritualism glories in its 'objective' phenomena—material movements, displacements of furniture, apparitions, cold draughts, noises, and vocal utterances. It has, in consequence, frequently been subject to the process of verification, although opinions are divided as to whether the phenomena have been verified or not. It is true that 'states of consciousness' cannot be directly verified, but nor can a great deal else. We cannot directly verify geological theories concerning the former condition of the earth's surface. They constitute a system of hypotheses by which we seek to account for the conditions which we can directly observe today. We cannot directly verify the accepted view as to the structure of the oxygen atom: it is a hypothesis that aims to interpret chemical phenomena that can be observed directly. We find no inconvenience in speaking of the 'state' of a piece of metal, for example when it is magnetized, although we infer the state only from the observed behaviour of the metal. The behaviorists cannot see that, where observation cannot penetrate, it is necessary to form a hypothesis. So necessary is it, that they introduce one while pretending not to do so; for the supposition that thought is really a form of muscular activity which escapes our observation is a hypothesis. But having rejected the theories of the metaphysicians, they display an irrational dread of all hypotheses. In this, as we can see from Gilbert Ryle's book, they are not alone.

Ryle's *The Concept of Mind* (London: Hutchinson, 1949) is an attempt to escape from the so-called psycho-physical problem by arguing that questions about the relation between body and mind are "improper questions". "My mind", he adds, "does not stand for another organ. It signifies my ability and proneness to do certain sorts of things and not some piece of personal apparatus without which I could or would not do them" (p. 168). But surely he knows that the brain is an organ without which a human being cannot function at all, and local injuries to which can curtail or abolish his "ability and proneness to do certain sorts of things". If the 'mind' is spoken of rather than the brain, it is because most people know their mental apparatus better from the psychological than from the anatomical aspect, just as they know their digestive system better from their feelings than from anatomical investigation. If there is really any objection to speaking of someone's mind, then there must be the same objection to speaking of his digestion. Those who refuse to allow such abstractions do not understand their usefulness. Ryle would probably think it as philosophically indecent to speak of a bullet and its velocity as of a body and its mind. He of course scorns the traditional distinctions of thought, feeling, and will as different aspects of mind (p. 62). But whether this analysis into cognition, emotion, and conation is adequate or not, it is certainly useful and therefore legitimate.

Let me try to illustrate such legitimate use of abstractions. It has long been fashionable to speak with contempt of those theorists who discussed some nonexistent entity which they called 'economic man' (man who always acts in his own economic interests), as if the use of any such abstractions were entirely inadmissible. But all science depends on their use. What could the zoologist do if he were to renounce the idea of dogs and cats and their specific characters and confine his studies to the idiosyncracies of Fido and Tibbs? What right has the geologist to talk of clay, limestone, granite, and gneiss, since there is no clay which is just clay? It is always some special kind with ingredients peculiar to itself. These individual differences are by no means unimportant. Had a particular lion on a particular occasion been less timid or more hungry, the career of Livingstone might have been cut short and the whole history of African colonization changed. Nevertheless, the zoologist continues to describe and discuss the average lion, the economic lion, and does anyone seriously expect him to do anything else?

In this question of what details may be neglected there are two opposed advantages to consider. When we establish a scientific law, we require 1. that it should correctly summarize the facts, and 2. that it should be simple enough for practical application. Taking a mathematical example, we obtain maximum simplicity by describing the path of a projectile as a parabola. This is accurate only if we neglect, for one thing, the effect of air resistance. We then allow for this resistance by saying that it is proportional to the projectile's velocity. This is more accurate than the first hypothesis, but is still inaccurate for high velocities. And so we proceed by gradually complicating our formula until we reach the last possible compromise between simplicity and accuracy. If the formula is too complex, it cannot be applied. If it does not approximate closely enough to the facts, it is useless. We build it up by degrees, taking first the simplest hypothesis which seems to correspond with the facts, seeing where it fits and where it fails, and then, as a result of such trials, modifying it. In this way the atomic theory was gradually built up from the simple beginnings of Democritus. A provisional formula is an essential means to the attainment of a better one. All this is fairly obvious in relation to the sciences of physics and chemistry. But the same kind of reasoning is appropriate in biological investigations.

When Ryle discusses the 'abilities' and 'pronenesses' which, for him, constitute mind, he argues that, because we can arrive at knowledge of them only by inference from visible and audible behaviour, they are in fact nothing but the sum total of such behaviour. On this view, there is no skill at chess, there are only skilful moves, no laziness but only lazy actions (p. 169). No psychological theory about the permanent or semipermanent condition underlying such behaviour is to be allowed: "When we describe people as exercising qualities of mind, we are not referring to occult episodes of which their overt acts and utterances are effects; we are referring to those overt acts and utterances themselves" (p. 25).

This contrast between 'occult' and 'overt' keeps recurring in Ryle's exposition, but his position is nevertheless not clear. If at one time he denies the existence of any concealed process in the mind, or in the head, at others he allows it.

It is surely obvious that when, for instance, we say that someone has wit, we are not simply saying the same as that on Tuesday last he made a crack at breakfast, and on Wednesday he did as much at dinner, and so on through the whole of his career; but from his past joking we infer a certain character or capacity which is conveniently called wit, and we expect from someone possessing such a capacity a certain type of behaviour. Ryle finds it quite impossible to sustain the view I have quoted him as propounding. Although according to this view conceit is only certain actions and modesty other actions, he has to admit that it is possible to be conceited and yet sham modesty in one's behaviour (p. 171). Hypocrites and shammers simulate qualities which they do not possess (pp. 172–73). But what is the meaning of this if there is no meaning to the word 'quality'? The traditional list of capacities, temperaments, and states of mind may well be inadequate, but we need to retain it until we can construct a better set of hypothetical states.

It may readily be granted that, whatever our notion of conceit, we judge a person by his words, expressions, and actions. In the same way the chemist judges the constitution and properties of a sample of salt, and the pathologist the character of a micro-organism, by observing reactions to his tests. But is it reasonable therefore to say that the salt is nothing but its reactions in the test-tube—that there is no 'occult' molecular structure underlying these—and the micro-coccus nothing but the staining reactions? Ryle supposes that any hypotheses about hidden goings on would do no more than enable us to observe the behaviour which we already in fact observe (p. 124). He cannot see that, although some hypotheses are thus barren, others, like the atomic theory, are extremely fertile, and that it is important for the scientist to be able to distinguish the two kinds. Very often, the behaviour of something can be much more accurately explained, predicted, and regulated by reference to its theoretical composition than by reference to its appearance as recorded in our memory. Such structural hypotheses serve to condense description and aid generalization. If we know that someone believes in ghosts, we have a useful clue to what he is likely to do in certain definite circumstances. If we know he is irascible, we cannot predict the specific acts he will perform on any particular occasion, but we do know what the general character of his behaviour is likely to be. The various emotions and thoughts we ascribe to human beings and to animals can serve as short ways of describing their probable behaviour.

Altogether, Ryle seems not to understand that, although an idea is based on forms and events observed and remembered, it is very much more than this. The world I conceive is very different from the world which I perceive. I conceive it as a continuous whole of which only fragments are perceptible to me. Observed aspects are supplemented, and they are not supplemented in the same way by every mind. That is why some people have more adequate and useful ideas than others. My idea of Ryle's state of mental confusion is not merely a catalogue of all his statements; and my judgement on this matter is not merely an induction from his words and sentences. It is in just such cases that we have to form hypotheses, and it is folly to deny psychology the right to do so. Because psychologists have been hampered by inadequate or ill-conceived hypotheses, that is no reason for saying that they must renounce hypotheses entirely.

That Ryle has inadequate views on the nature of ideas is further suggested by the way he exaggerates the importance of language in the thinking process. He certainly suggests that 'talk' is an important, if not the prime ingredient in intellectual activity. He believes—surely quite erroneously—that children do not theorize at all before they go to school, where "the techniques of theorizing are learned in set lessons" (p. 185). I have argued that even perception involves theorizing, and young children are capable of quite obvious theorizing. A friend can recall that, at the age of three, he supposed that an 18-year-old cousin he was meeting for the first time must be very old because she was very tall. For Ryle, however, "intellectual tasks are those or some of those which only the schooled can perform"; intellectual accomplishments are "exploitations of lessons learned at least in part from books and lectures, or, in general, from didactic discourse"; and "intellectual talk is edified or edifying talk" (p. 284). Such can be the pompousness of the philosopher.

In some passages he even commits himself to the view that thought is not possible without language: "Thinking things out involves saying things to oneself, or to one's other companions, with instructive intent" (p. 313). Yet this is not his overall position, and in a volume of essays published posthumously he expressly repudiates it.[1] He nevertheless believes, with the Logical Positivists, that logical principles may be inferred from what he calls "the logical behaviour of terms" (p. 126), from the "habits" of words and the conventions of language. For him it is in any context a sufficient argument that a particular form of words does or does not 'make sense', by which he means that it is, or is not, a form commonly used.

It is Ryle's endless illustrations of habitual usage that make his book read like the totally uncontrolled chatter of an incurable gossip; for there is, in general, little or no indication of what it is that such examples exemplify. Here, for example, is what he says about "dispositional statements": many of them

> may be, though they need not be, and ordinarily are not, expressed with the help of the words 'can', 'could' and 'able'. 'He is a swimmer', when it does not signify that he is an expert, means merely that he can swim. But the words 'can' and 'able' are used in lots of different ways, as can be illustrated by the following examples. 'Stones can float (for pumice-stone floats)'; 'that fish can swim (for it is not disabled, although it is now inert in the mud)'; 'John Doe can swim (for he has learned and not forgotten)'; 'Richard Doe can swim (if he is willing to learn)'; 'you can swim (when you try hard)'; 'she can swim (for the doctor has withdrawn his veto)' and so on. The first example . . . (pp. 126–27).

He then proceeds to explain the meanings of the word 'can'. Then, as if he were not quite sure that his readers had followed him, he adds:

> To bring out the different forces of some of these different uses of 'can' and 'able', it is convenient to make a brief disquisition on the logic of what are sometimes called the 'modal words', such as 'can', 'must', 'may', 'is necessarily', 'is not necessarily' and 'is not necessarily not'.

This is the kind of thing involved in such a "disquisition":

> A statement to the effect that something must be, or is necessarily, the case functions as what I have called an 'inference-ticket'; it licenses the inference to the thing's being the case from something else which may or may not be specified in the statement. When the statement is to the effect that something is necessarily not, or cannot be, the case, it functions as a licence to infer to its not being the case. Now sometimes it is required to refuse such a licence to infer that something is not the case, and we commonly word this refusal by saying that it can be the case, or that it is possibly the case. To say that something can be the case does not entail that it is the case, or that it is not the case, or, of course, that it is in suspense between being and not being the case, but only that there is no licence to infer from something else, specified or unspecified, to its not being the case. (p. 127)

He asks us to accept these trivial observations on the uses of a common word as a "general account" of the "logic" of modal words.

Keith Ward was understandably horrified to find that Ryle, his tutor, supposed himself qualified to write about mind simply, as Ward says, by "assembling and analysing some of the concepts we use in ordinary speech", in total ignorance of psychology.[2] But worse still is Ryle's conviction that the meaning of words can be ascertained just by studying the contexts in which they are correctly used. He says:

> A word and its meaning are not two things that I acquire when I learn the word, for all

that learning its meaning certainly is learning more than its pronunciation and spelling. . . . The word is not a noise *and* something else as well; and it is not just a noise. It is a complexly qualified noise, a noise endowed with a quite specific *saying*-power, endowed sometimes by institutional regulations, generally by accumulating public custom, slightly rigorized by pedagogic disciplines. (1979, p. 88)

In truth, "institutional regulations", "public custom" and other conventions concerning usage do not in themselves disclose the meanings of words. To some people the word 'ruminant' means merely a creature that ruminates. To better informed persons it means a good deal more. On the other hand, there must be many who have learned to say that a cow is a ruminant without ever discovering what the process of ruminating consists in. What connection there is between words and things and words and ideas has to be ascertained additionally to the words, by reference to these non-verbal realities. Apart from the thoughts behind the words, language would be as meaningless as the noise of a typewriter; and it is often by no means easy to ascertain what these thoughts are.

There are, however, passages in Ryle's *The Concept of Mind* which allow that thought is not necessarily linked with language, and which read like a statement of more acceptable views of wherein thinking consists—as when he says that people may "formulate their thoughts in diagrams and pictures" and "do not always set these out on paper", but " 'see them in their minds' eyes' ". He writes in this connection of "an internal cinematograph show of visual imagery" (p. 27). There follows a long discussion about "knowing how" and "knowing that", the object of which is to prove that a skill may be acquired without first acquiring a theoretical formula, that someone may play chess skilfully without running over in his head all the relevant rules and tactical maxims of the game in advance. Ryle is here contesting what he calls "the absurd assumption made by the intellectualist legend", namely "that a performance of any sort inherits all its title to intelligence from some anterior internal operation of planning what to do". He does not deny that "very often we do go through such a process of planning"; but he finds it unwarranted to suppose that, "for an operation to be intelligent, it must be steered by a prior intellectual operation" (pp. 31–32). But this is surely just what is meant by intelligent behaviour. When an animal does *not* know how to deal with the situation confronting him, he is likely to perform his repertoire of reactions until he chances on one which meets the case. Thereafter he may use this response at once when the same situation recurs, but for every new situation he resorts to similar actual physical experiment in order to find the proper reply. Intelligent behaviour, however, consists in running through possible responses to a novel situation in the imagination, instead of actually performing them, and then selecting the right response before making any outward trial or movement at all. Köhler's experiments, recorded in his classic *The Mentality of Apes,* were largely concerned to demonstrate that these animals are capable of such behaviour, and it is hard to accept the truth of his record and doubt this. They can think of and then construct a desired situation as when they seek and find a tool which puts bananas within reach, or build up a material standing ground (for instance by fetching boxes and placing one upon another) from which they can reach their goal. The effectiveness of such thinking depends on the existence in the memory of the elements into which previous experiences have been analysed. Actions and situations are both composite; large and complex situations, and complex series of actions may be retained in the memory, but they are of use in this type of thinking only if similar situations are likely to recur. To cope with novel situations, previous experiences must be analyzed into elements and these assembled into new complexes. Hence if past experience is to enable the animal to respond to a situation with a suitable series of actions, he must know of each element in his behaviour—not whether it was successful or otherwise in various quite different circumstances, but what its precise effects were; for only thus can the combined effects of the components of his intended action be estimated and compared with the actual situation. In this way, a complex action is thought out and resolved upon which has never been performed as a whole before; but it is made up of a small number of phases which, although now combined for the first time, have separately occurred perhaps often.

In combining remembered elements to construct a new situation, the effort of construction becomes greater in proportion to the number of elements to be combined. Man is able to contrive more complex plans from the elements of his experience than the chimpanzee, and so he both achieves much more and also makes much more serious mistakes.

In a later essay Ryle shows himself aware of

the importance of imaginative thinking of this kind. To cross an unbridged watercourse, he says, "we have to think up for ourselves and then suspiciously try out possible ways of getting where we want to be". In such a situation "we do not know what to do until we have thought what to do" (1979, pp. 56–57). Yet if one supposes, as he and Russell do, that ideas can be expressed in words or in a picture of a single aspect of an object or situation, or in mathematical or other tables, then there is nothing of importance for the silent mental apparatus to perform that cannot be performed as well or better in speech or writing.

Behaviorism was not, in the first instance, specially concerned with language, and came to assign importance to it because of the necessity of finding something to take over the traditional duties of the 'mind', which was no longer recognized in behaviorist psychology. It has done much to resuscitate Condillac's doctrine that science is merely a language well-arranged. Different scientific ideas and hypotheses are today often referred to as if they were merely different ways of talking. But language is not something which we can manipulate and experiment with in our minds in such a way as to be sure of making reliable inferences to reality from the results of such experiments. When we plan an outing, it is sometimes easier to think in terms of a map rather than of the actual topography. This is because the map has been constructed in such a way that there is a dependable correlation between distances on it and distances on the actual ground, between contours on it and gradients in the terrain, and between the position of conventional symbols on it, indicating footpaths, roads, railways, and so forth, and the exact location of these things in the area. There is no such rigid correlation between words on the one hand and ideas and things on the other.

II. Chomsky

The chief objection made to the theory of the behaviorists was not the fundamental one that it failed to give any adequate explanation of animal behaviour, but that it seemed to reduce man to something little better than an automaton, and clearly reduced all psychology to a simple matter of stimulus and response. All religion and philosophy were made into a mere series of imperceptible laryngeal twitchings, no more significant than the creaking of a door. It is not surprising that efforts were made to save the soul, the mind, the spirit, by some means, and it is evident that the theorizings of Chomsky were prompted by this ambition. In his *Cartesian Linguistics,* he recalls the view of Descartes on the function of the soul and its habitation in the brain. In the same book he quotes the views of some late eighteenth- and early nineteenth-century writers on language—Herder, Schlegel, Humboldt—all of whom support his view that language is something uniquely human and is related to the soul. He refers to these writers with apparent approval, without however stating clearly that he adopts their theories. That the value of any support they give on the subject is highly questionable is something that I have tried to show elsewhere.[3]

In the *Times Literary Supplement* of 18–24 August, 1989, Gilbert Harman declared that

Chomsky "may well turn out to be the Galileo of the science of mind" (p. 898). Chomsky himself supposes that his investigations "suggest that all current approaches to problems of perception and organization of behavior suffer from a failure to attribute sufficient depth and complexity to the mental processes that must be represented in any model that attempts to come to grips with the empirical phenomena". He adds that lack of space does not allow him "a detailed development of these topics"—otherwise he would presumably be able to enlighten us on the "potential significance" of "phonological structure" for "cognitive psychology" (L and M, p. 32).[4] That is to say, given space, he could show that something about the way people think and reason can be explained by a study of the way in which sounds are combined to produce words. He has a peculiar way of expressing himself, and writes of "setting linguistic theory within the general framework of the study of human intellectual capacities and their specific character" (CI, pp. 25–26). This presumably means explaining language by reference to human psychology in general. But it is hard to imagine any rational alternative to this.

These claims that linguistics can illuminate the thinking process seem not to have been highly regarded in some quarters, for Harman records that "today. . . . most cognitive scientists outside linguistics think of linguistics as uninteresting and irrelevant". He claims, however, that "very many brilliant investigators" have followed up Chomsky's work in a way that "has led to many new insights about how languages are the same and how they differ". What these insights are he does not tell us, not even in outline, as "the subject has become quite complex". A less sympathetic observer might hold that this is largely due to the way its practitioners introduce technical terms, each one of which is defined in terms of others which are themselves unclear. As an example, I mention Chomsky's statements that a "formative" is a "string of minimal syntactically functioning elements", and that "strings of formatives" are "generated" by the "syntactic component" which "specifies the categories, functions and structural interrelations of the formatives and systems of formatives" (CI, p. 9). These statements do not throw any light on the meaning of any one of the terms that compose it until all the rest have been explained. As one reads on, the vocabulary of unclear terms reaches formidable dimensions. It is an interesting fact that whenever I have consulted some admirer of Chomsky for help in understanding what he is driving at, they always refer me to the works of other writers and never undertake any elucidation themselves. It is an equally interesting fact that others have had similar experiences.[5]

Speech is a form of behaviour which cannot be shown to differ in any fundamental way from other forms. Chomsky bases his belief to the contrary on what he calls the "creative" function of language, by which he means that we can utter and understand a very large number of different sentences even though we have never spoken or heard them before. "Most of our linguistic experience", he says, "both as speakers and hearers, is with new sentences" (CI, p. 7); in his own next sentence he changes "new" to "entirely new". This is absurd. If any passage of normal English is broken up into phrases or short groups of words, it will be found that novelty is the exception rather than the rule. It is only the combination that is new, and this is true of Chomsky's own writing (even though he goes out of his way to introduce jargon), as we can see from a few of the phrases he uses on p. 8 of CI:

> a factor of minute importance
>
> most of them, on the contrary, are composed
>
> one of the fundamental errors
>
> developed by a follower along these lines
>
> in any event
>
> is only of marginal interest
>
> each normal human

Not only our speech, but all our actions are subject to an equally large number of combinations of basic elements. No cricket or tennis player performs the same series of strokes whenever he plays. Even walking, running, or jumping means adapting one's movements to the terrain, so that it is unlikely that these will be exactly the same on different occasions. The relevant muscular movements are familiar enough, but they will have to be differently combined, just as the behaviour of other animals is an ever novel combination of basic components, as the animal adapts his actions to the external situation.[6] We are apt to assume that two actions are identical if we give them the same name. But the horse that jumps a fence must adapt his muscular efforts to the size of the fence and the nature of the ground from which he takes off. The dog that chews a bone must adapt movements of jaws and tongue to the shape and size of the bone, and for no two successive bones can he follow the same sequence.

Chomsky cannot believe that we learn our language by hearing people talk and trying to convey our thoughts to them because he supposes that this would mean learning every possible word and word-group by frequent repetition, and with some kind of 'reinforcement' (reward for success) and punishment for failure. Such a way of learning would seem to exclude any possibility of concocting a *new* sentence, one that had not been acquired by the process of frequent repetition. In fact, human beings are capable of learning from a single experience, and do not even need an immediate reward, still less a series of such 'reinforcements'. They can also learn by imitation. All learning depends on trial and error. Someone has learned a language when he can make the necessary noises to influence other persons who speak the same language. A child must experiment with his vocal organs until he finds how to do this. He may at first say 'tooths' instead of 'teeth', or, having been told that certain animals are 'oxen', will identify others as 'sheepen'. It is not only children who make this kind of mistake by basing their practice on analogy. The process in more sophisticated cases is called premature generalization, and is to be met with at every turn in human and (as we shall see) in other mammalian behaviour.

The best excuse for Chomsky is the obvious absurdity of the behaviorist account of what is involved in learning a language. Bloomfield, for instance, who supposes that "thinking is talking to oneself", explains learning to speak by supposing that the child makes vocal noises which he repeats and hears: "this results in a habit: whenever a similar sound strikes his ear, he is likely to make these same mouth-movements".[7] In fact, however, the power to recognize any object—word or thing—and separate it from its background involves two kinds of learning process: on the one hand the different aspects of the object must be associated together so as to form an idea of the object, and on the other hand each of these aspects must be separated from all the various aspects of situations in which they may be presented. "The dog, for example, must not only learn to recognize the cat's figure from every point of view; he must also learn to discern each of these projections against many different backgrounds".[8] A word may present different aspects, in that it is pronounced in different ways: in a high pitch by the child's mother, and in a low pitch by its father; and it can be sung, shouted, or whispered by either. It also occurs in different contexts. The difference between individual aspects is even greater when it is written. W.R. Brain observes:

> We have learned to recognize a word whether it is printed in one kind of type or another, whether the letters are large or small, and in all the variety of individual calligraphies, provided that the handwriting is not completely illegible. . . . Therefore, if we are to recognize as a single word all the possible variants of visual symbols in which it can be printed or written, they must possess in common the power of evoking the same central word-scheme already established in the process of learning to talk.[9]

We have not, to my knowledge, been told, even by Chomsky, that we learn to read because we possess some kind of knowledge of writing before birth, and that there is no conceivable way in which a child could discover how to read merely from the words he sees. And reading is but an example of what is involved in learning generally: all the different aspects of an object must, in Brain's terminology, 'possess in common the power of evoking the same central schema' in the brain. Clearly, any animal has some inborn capacity that enables him to learn what he is capable of learning. But he still has to go through the process of learning. In the case of children learning a language, the process depends on what Colin Blakemore has called "continuous and lengthy lessons."[10]

A child learns to connect a word with a thing by association. Sometimes he will extend the application of a word, contrary to the normal usage, because of some resemblance, as when the proper name of a dog or cat is transferred to other members of the species. He has to learn that sometimes a word is used for a variety of things which differ a good deal from one another, sometimes only for a number of very similar things, and occasionally for one thing only. He learns that 'Fido' means just one particular dog, that 'donkey' means many distinct but similar creatures, that 'flower' stands for a great variety of things, some of which resemble each other very little, and that the word 'thing' has an almost completely indefinite meaning. There is nothing in the word itself to tell him the extent to which its meaning varies. The child learns phrases as well as words: indeed, he has no means of distinguishing the two until he begins to write or has learned enough to be able to recognize which sound-groups are inseparable and which can be broken up into parts that can be recombined into fresh groups. He may associate these sounds with actions or situations, not only with objects. Although he may recognize the difference between the idea of an object and the idea of an action, this has nothing to do with grammar; for actions can be designated by nouns, and verbs—for instance the two commonest verbs in English, 'to be' and 'to have'—do not necessarily denote actions.

The first step towards grammar consists in stringing a few words together to convey an idea which no single word is available to express. It is quite gratuitous to suppose that the child has an innate consciousness of some kind of grammatical rules which tells him what constructions are acceptable. It has been pointed out that the physiology of the brain does not suggest that grammatical rules are established before language is actually required.[11] Yet Chomsky's theories imply that something like this is the case; for he believes that our ability to learn the language of our parents or guardians when we are very young can be explained only if we are born with an intuitive knowledge of fundamental rules of speech common to all languages. There must, so he thinks, be some inherited system of grammatical and syntactical rules, more general than those which apply to any particular language, but just as definite. He is not prepared to accept the view that it is the common terrestrial environment, the characters which are common to the vocal organs of all races, and the common needs of human beings which account for whatever is common to all languages.

In view of the difficulty of establishing satisfactory rules even for English, it is not surprising to find Chomsky admitting that "discovering the principles of universal grammar that interweave with the rules of particular grammars to provide explanations for phenomena that appear arbitrary and chaotic" is "the most challenging theoretical problem in linguistics" (L and M, p. 40). The rules he concocts for English are complicated enough, and he writes of their "cyclic application" (L and M, p. 38). This means that, if rule no. 1 does not fit, you apply rule no. 2, and if that does not work you have rule no. 3 up your sleeve, and so on. The extreme complexity of the rules if exceptions are not to be admitted is one of the things on which he relies for his theory that no process of learning could ever enable someone to speak in accordance with them. They must therefore be innate, and obviously unique to man.

From these premisses Chomsky is not willing to conclude that the formation of derivatives in English (e.g. 'signify' from 'sign') is determined by convention. He devotes some pages of L and M (pp. 33ff) to suggesting rules for forming them. One can only hope that, if such a book of rules is ever compiled, it will never find its way into schools. He is at pains to explain why the stressed syllable in the adjective 'righteous', formed from the noun 'right', is pronounced in the same way as in this noun, whereas this is not so with 'contrition', derived from 'contrite', nor with 'ignition', from 'ignite' (It is because 'righteous' derives from a form in which there was another consonant, represented now by *gh*, but no longer pronounced). He does not tell us why 'might' does not form the adjective 'mighteous' and 'light' 'lighteous', but no doubt further rules could be adduced to explain this. It would also be interesting to know why we get 'explanation' from 'explain', but not 'disdanation' and 'complanation' from 'disdain' and 'complain'. And as we have 'derivation', why not also 'contrivation', 'revivation', 'survivation', and so forth? The same medley of convention determines the use of suffixes which modify in a fairly constant way the meaning of the noun to which they are affixed. We say 'priceless', but not (except perhaps facetiously) 'bookless', 'clockless'. 'Harmless' and 'useless' correspond to 'harmful' and 'useful', but 'noiseless' and 'profitless' have no counterparts with -ful; instead we say 'noisy' and 'profitable'. Idioms, as well as individual words, are likewise determined by custom, not by any profound psychological laws. As for pronunciation, such partial rules as there are (with their numerous exceptions) have surely come about because, when a new word is formed, its pronunciation is determined partly by ease, partly by analogy with words that resemble it in some way, and (if the language exists in written form) partly by spelling. Two otherwise identical words can be distinguished by being accented differently, as 'contráct' and 'cóntract' (verb and noun), similarly with 'contrast', 'consort', 'convict', 'converse'. But the rule is not invariable, and we have 'contról' for both verb and noun, as also with 'repose', 'report', 'reprieve', 'neglect', and so on.

Chomsky discusses "pronominalisation", by which he means substituting a pronoun for a noun, and tries to account for the fact that this cannot be done with every sentence. What he is asserting as an explanation of this restriction is far from clear. The naive and surely correct view is that it should not be done if it gives rise to ambiguity, and that this depends on two principal things: 1. the context (including the whole real as well as verbal situation) in which the relevant sentence occurs, and its meaning; and 2. whether or not some clue is given as to the meaning of the pronoun by what has been said or written before. In conversation the general situation is the more important factor, in writing the second point is the chief one. In conversation 'he's done it again' may present the hearer with no difficulty in identifying both doer and deed; in writing it will probably be necessary to specify who has done what. It is astonishing that anyone who has made a serious study of language should suppose that rules can be drawn up without reference to *meaning* and *context.*

It is because Chomsky under-rates the importance of meaning that what he stresses in a language is not its vocabulary, but its grammar and syntax, and it is these with which his illustrations are mainly concerned. Here he is clearly beholden to Humboldt, who investigated a number of what he regarded as primitive languages and compared them to the ideal language (Greek). Finding an absence of inflections, and discovering that these languages seemed to get on without them, he began to speculate on what he called the 'form' of language, as opposed to its vocabulary.[12] It is, however, the vocabulary that is most burdensome on the memory (as one rapidly discovers when one tries to learn a language), and also the most important, as it is necessary to be able to give to every object, event, or action a name which is associated in the mind of one's hearer with the same object, event, or action. Grammar and syntax are less important, since many people—not only foreigners—speak ungrammatically and yet are able to make themselves understood. It is far more important to know the meaning of the words than to put them into grammatically correct statements, and some people never achieve grammatical correctness. According to Chomsky, no rules are required for incorrect speech. The convenience of this principle does not need to be emphasized. If we do in fact inherit some underlying knowledge of grammatical rules, then, as Englefield notes, "it is surprising how many people learn at an early age to suppress their inherited tendencies".[13]

Chomsky claims that sentences can be recognized as grammatical or not apart from their meaning. He tries to demonstrate this by arguing that even a nonsense sentence, such as "Colourless green ideas sleep furiously" is immediately recognized as grammatical, whereas "furiously sleep ideas green colourless" is at once seen to be a muddle. Now he must assume that the reader knows the common meanings of the individual words, for he surely would not undertake to decide whether a sequence of Chinese words was grammatical or not unless he was well acquainted with the Chinese language. The grammatical features in the sentence he has constructed must lie in the order of the words and in their form (inflections, suffixes, and so forth). The only inflection is the 's' of 'ideas'. But many English words end in 's' ('speaks', 'appears'), and we can recognize this 's' as a sign of the plural only because we know the word 'idea' and its meaning. His sentence includes two suffixes, -less and -ly, and the former generally denotes an adjective, the latter an adverb. However, -ly cannot be recognized as a suffix unless we know the meaning of the relevant word, as it can also terminate words when it is not a suffix (tally, rally, folly, holly, etc.). Furthermore, even as a suffix it does not invariably denote an adverb, but can be used to change a noun into an adjective (manly, shapely, godly, deathly, friendly, etc.). 'Green' can be a noun in English, but as it here precedes what we know, from its meaning, to be a noun, we understand it as an adjective. There is nothing to show that 'sleep' is a verb except its position after the noun 'ideas'. But it is by no means an invariable rule that adjectives precede the noun they qualify, or that verbs must follow their subjects in affirmative sentences. We might say 'down came the rain', and it would be quite possible to add a couple of adjectives. Hence 'green' can be understood as an adjective and 'sleep' as a verb only because we know what they mean. If we do not know the meaning of the words, all that we can infer from their form is that the first word of the sentence is an adjective and the last probably an adverb. And so it is not because of the lack of grammar that the other sentence is a meaningless jumble, but because the first sentence does not make sense. If we take another short sentence of the same grammatical form as Chomsky's (adjective, adjective, noun, verb, adverb):

Wise young students work assiduously *or*

Ambitious American professors theorize incoherently

it will not be difficult to decipher the meaning in whatever order the words are written.

I do not mean to suggest that word-order is of no importance. Since there is order in the world, in trying to describe any portion of it—either by pictures, diagrams, maps, gestures, or common speech—we must, in our representation, include some kind of order to represent the order in what we are describing. Order is thus important in all forms of communication. In a painting or photograph we have a two-dimensional representation of a three-dimensional reality. In a map we have the same, although here we use a number of conventions and omit nearly all the details. In spoken language we must be content with what is possible with a single dimension—a series of words, each one of which represents part of the complex reality—and the order of the words can show the relations between the various words of the sentence. Words whose meaning is closely related in the proposition can be connected in the verbal expression, either by being placed in close proximity, or by some form of grammatical agreement, as in Latin. In good, simple English or French, nouns are placed close to the adjectives which qualify them, either immediately before or immediately after; the subject of the verb is placed as close as possible to the verb, as are also the adverbs. Prepositions are put immediately before the noun with which they are connected in meaning. Where subordinate clauses take the place of noun or adjective, the same general principle applies, but compromises are often necessary when different elements compete for the same position. The writer or speaker shows his skill by arranging his words so as best to satisfy these general requirements, and it is as a result of them that the rules with which Chomsky is so concerned have grown up. We all learn from reading and listening how to frame our sentences to best advantage.

At one point Chomsky almost apologizes for paying so little attention to the effect of the meaning of the words on the construction of the sentences which they can form, although he avoids the word 'meaning' and speaks here instead of "semantic interpretation":

> In discussing the nature of grammatical operations, I have restricted myself to syntactic and phonological examples, avoiding questions of semantic interpretation. If a grammar is to characterize the full linguistic competence of the speaker-hearer, it must comprise rules of semantic interpretation as well, but little is known of any depth regarding this aspect of grammar. (L and M, p. 49)

This concedes that a useful grammar should supplement the dictionary of a language by supplying rules for the modification and arrangement of words in sentences so as to express intelligible ideas in, as far as possible, an unambiguous way, and in accordance with the established conventions of the people whose native language it is. It is hard to see how Chomsky's researches are likely to be helpful as a contribution to the construction of such a grammar for any language, for on the next page he confesses himself "unable to discuss" rules that make reference to the meaning of the words—"rules of semantic interpretation that might be analogous" to the "syntactic and phonological rules mentioned earlier". The operations he has been discussing in relation to syntax have all involved some alteration in the order of the words of a sentence. But if one tries to construct rules for word-order without reference to the meaning of the words, they are bound to be quite unhelpful. One might, for instance, say:

> i. to make a sentence negative, put the

longest word first, the second longest
second, and so on.

ii. to turn a sentence into a question, put
the last word first, the next to last
second, and so on.

iii. to make a sentence into a relative
clause, put the words in alphabetical
order.

By changing the order in accordance with such
rules, we should contravene the one valid rule
which must apply to all forms of communication,
namely that the linkage which exists between the
things referred to or the ideas expressed must be
symbolized in some manner by the arrangement
of the elements of the communication.

Chomsky and others have tried to formulate
what they call "transformational rules" for con-
verting ordinary (or "surface") grammatical structure into a supposed underlying "deep structure".
He believes that the deep structure of a sentence
consists of a series of propositions: "A system of
propositions expressing the meaning of a sentence is produced in the mind as the sentence is
realized as a physical signal, the two being related
by certain formal operations that, in current terminology, we may call *grammatical transformations*" (L and M, p. 25). His idea is that, to be
understood, every idiomatic expression must be
rephrased—quite unconsciously, of course—
into a form that is logically and grammatically
faultless and free from all ambiguity. It is common knowledge that, in English and probably in
most languages, an idea can be expressed in
more than one way. If we take what John Lyons
calls "one of Chomsky's most famous examples",[14] namely 'Flying planes can be dangerous',

this may mean that flying a plane is dangerous work, or that planes are dangerous if (or when) in flight. The first meaning could be rendered with:

> To fly a plane is dangerous.
>
> Plane-flying is dangerous.
>
> A pilot's work is dangerous.

And, for the second, we might say:

> Air-borne planes are a source of danger.
>
> A plane is dangerous once it has taken off.
>
> A falling plane can do much damage.

Anyone who takes a little trouble when putting his ideas into writing is aware of such choice of expressions and uses the form of words which is least likely to be misunderstood. But to suppose that every sentence has one particular form—a proposition or a series of propositions—which represents the meaning precisely, that this perfect form exists in some mysterious way at the back of the speaker's mind, and that, in order to understand him, the hearer must translate his words back into this ideal form, is obviously not true. Yet this is what is implied by the theory of surface and deep structure. The deep structure, says Chomsky, is "the underlying abstract structure" that "determines the semantic interpretation" (the meaning) of the sentence. Thus "to account for the normal use of language we must attribute to the speaker-hearer an intricate system of rules that involve mental operations of a very abstract nature" (CL, pp. 33–34, L and M, pp. 52–53). In actual fact, however, it is the material situation, the relationship between speaker and listener, their common experience, and the circumstances of the moment which give a sentence its meaning, and given these conditions there is no ambiguity in a phrase such as 'flying planes'. If it were necessary for the hearer to translate every sentence into a "disambiguated" form of words before he could understand what was said, communication would be slower and more uncertain than it is.

In a later publication, Chomsky withdraws some of his claims for deep structures, saying that they "do not play the role formerly attributed to them" and that "a suitably enriched notion of surface structure suffices to determine the meaning of sentences under interpretive rules". Nevertheless, he adds, these deep structures ("initial phrase markers" as he here also calls them) do "enter, though now indirectly into determining the structures that undergo semantic interpretation"—they do still influence the grammatical form of ordinary sentences which mean something. On the one hand, then, he admits that surface structure can be understood without first being transposed into deep structure. Yet he cannot bring himself to abandon this latter chimera entirely, and so reserves for it an "indirect" role, and still claims that it has "significant and revealing properties."[15]

When we speak to one another, we take for granted a vast amount of knowledge common to speaker and listener, and as a rule our statements need consist of little more than hints. If the general drift of a writer is clear, there is no need to be perplexed by the occasional use of a wrong word. Mrs Malaprop had no difficulty in making herself understood. If two people, by similar experiences, have formed very similar ideas, then it will as a rule be easy for either to evoke his own idea in the mind of the other by very brief verbal formulas, and conversation between people with a certain range of ideas in common may be easy. But such people do not *express* their ideas in words, they merely hint at them, suggest them, just as with a wink or a gesture we may convey quite extensive information to a confederate who has preknowledge of what we are likely to wish to convey to him. A man says to his wife: 'The jug is broken'. From his tone of voice, the look on his face, and the fact that he has just been washing up, she knows at once that it is the precious piece inherited from her grandmother. Yet without the attendant circumstances, the proposition would convey nothing. With them it represents a whole complex of ideas, shared by these two persons, and because this complex is thus shared, the brief formula can transmit it.

In any case, precise and comprehensive representation in words even of a simple real event is impossible. Even in the most restricted field, it is not possible to have a special name for every element and component, every conceivable combination, every aspect that may need to be referred to; and for two reasons: first that the memory would fail, and second that one cannot know in advance everything that one may have need to mention. But if the nature of the event is known to the listener, the speaker has only to indicate it by a gesture or a phrase in order to convey what is required. The ambiguity of many of the commonest words would be fatal were it not for the fact that communication takes place in a common environment and context, and it is this real (as well as verbal) context which removes most of the ambiguities. 'He took out a . . . ' What did he take out? A revolver, a licence, a tooth? The meaning of the verb differs in each case, but the context suffices to make clear what is meant—not only the verbal context, but the real context formed by our knowledge of the relation between a man and his weapons, between client and official, and between dentist and patient.[16]

It follows that precise rules for avoidance of ambiguity are unnecessary. Such grammatical rules as exist are the result of imitation, generalization, and practical experience. Since a very large number of people contribute to the determination of these rules, they all have numerous exceptions, and they change to some extent from generation to generation. The practice of writing, and the preservation of numerous specimens of language in writing, is a conservative influence, but new words and phrases are continually being introduced, and analogy plays a part in determining their form. To suggest that the forms of language can be reduced to a precise system of rules is chimerical.

Just how chimerical appears from Lyons's discussion of framing rules to eliminate ambiguities. He mentions the phrase "eating apples" and thinks that one possible meaning could be 'apples which eat'. As apples do not eat, there are obvious objections to this interpretation. But Lyons, like Chomsky whom he admires and in many respects follows, is concerned with grammar, and if we are to be able to say that this interpretation is ungrammatical, we need some rule to exclude it. Hence we need to know "whether the noun *apple* and the verb *eat* are subclassified in the lexicon (by means of grammatical 'features' . . .) in such a way that the grammatical rules will admit or prohibit the combination of a noun with a given 'feature' (e.g. [inanimate]) as the subject of the verb-class of which *eat* is a member" (p. 253). The idea seems to be this. There are some sentences which, according to the traditional rules, are quite grammatical, yet unacceptable because they make nonsense, for instance:

> Bees fry sausages.

> Roses envy lilies.

> Blankets sing carols.

The words 'bees', 'roses', 'blankets', will be 'classified' in the lexicon: the whole vocabulary of nouns will be arranged in categories 1, 2, 3 . . . and so on. Similarly, the verbs will be classified as 1v, 2v, 3v . . . , and the grammar book will contain rules stating which classes of nouns can be used as subjects or objects of which classes of verbs. Thus one rule might be: any noun in category 7 may be used with any verb in 9v, 25v, . . . and so on. When we have a complete set of rules, we shall be able to talk sense without necessarily knowing what we are saying: grammar will have been made independent of sense. Since there would clearly have to be a very large number of rules, it might seem that our present method of deciding what sentences are 'acceptable' is a good deal more satisfactory.

To draw up such a list of rules would be a formidable task. On a single page of the *Concise Oxford Dictionary* we meet the nouns: shoveller, show, shower, shrapnel, shred, shrew. To find out what verbs can form predicates to these subjects we must go through a list of all the verbs in the dictionary. Taking 'shrapnel', we may, for example, say that shrapnel fills the shell, lies on the ground, wounds the soldier, penetrates the heart, and so on. Can we now put all these verbs into the same category? And is there any other noun that would fit the same verbal category?

There is a common English expression 'to take the opportunity', which corresponds to the French 'profiter de l'occasion' and the German 'die Gelegenheit ergreifen', and which has, no doubt, equivalents in most other languages, since situations in which the expression is appropriate are common enough everywhere. It means that, in order to do A, I have to be in the situation S, and that, as I should have to get myself into the same situation S if I wanted to do B, I might as well do B now while I am in the situation S, instead of having the trouble of getting myself into the situation S again, more especially as I know that I shall need to do B sooner or later, and there is no reason why I should not do it now. One might suppose from recent writers on linguistics that, in order to understand what anybody means who uses the phrase, I must first spell it out mentally into something like this rigmarole. In fact, however, the idea of opportunity involves and includes all this, and can affect my behaviour as soon as it arises in my mind, without my first working it out in a series of causal and conditional statements. The 'surface structure' of the relevant 'utterance' evokes the idea directly, and not via some queer periphrasis derived by exponents of linguistics. And how many thousands of expressions could we not find to illustrate the same point! The idea of opportunity can, of course, arise without hearing or thinking of any words, in the face of innumerable familiar situations which, though complicated to describe in words, are instantly recognized as exploitable; as a result, we can respond appropriately with the very minimum of delay.

It is possible both to think and to make statements, in the sense of conveying information, without recourse to verbal language at all. The flying of a flag can amount to a statement, so can the ringing of a bell, the pouting of the lips, or indeed any kind of signal. Chomsky does not go so far as to equate thinking with speech. He comes very close to doing so in his *Cartesian Linguistics* where—as Vivian Salmon justly notes in her lengthy review—he implies that linguistic and mental processes are virtually identical.[17] (If this is so, then the meaning of a sentence is simply another sentence.) He begins that work by welcoming (p. 3) the view of Descartes, who, quite wrongly, regarded all animal behaviour and much of human behaviour as mechanical (explicable in mechanistic terms), and reserved for man the power of thought.[18] And Descartes did at times express the view that language is the sole evidence for this power.[19] It is a short step from this to make language the essence of all reasoning and hence to give supreme importance to the task of analysing language. Chomsky's apparent endorsement of the views of Descartes suggests that he is ready to regard all animal behaviour as purely reflex, whereas he supposes human speech to be "stimulus-free" (CL, pp. 6, 77). If this means entirely undetermined, then it is not true. What someone says at any moment is determined by his inherited character, his experience, and the situation in which he happens to be. That we cannot specify and enumerate all the conditions does not mean that they do not exist, and if we call such behaviour stimulus-free because we cannot predict precisely at any moment what a person will say, we must call a great deal of animal behaviour stimulus-free for the same reason. Chomsky's concern to provide an antidote to the "anti-mentalism" of behaviorism has made him into something of a champion of the human soul. Psychology is the one branch of science that still has to contend with religious prejudice. The belief in the soul, that mysterious invisible something which dwells in the body while life lasts and departs at the moment of death, is incorporated in most religious systems, which can use it both as a promise of immortality and as a threat of punishment in an afterlife. The flat earth, Adam's rib, and Noah's ark have all been given up as expendable in consequence of various scientific discoveries, but belief in an immortal soul is not so readily abandoned.

The subtitle of Chomsky's *Cartesian Linguistics* is "A Chapter in the History of Rationalist Thought". 'Rationalism' here means the doctrine that our ideas are derived from the reason, not from experience, and in this sense it is opposed to 'empiricism'. Chomsky's belief that the fundamentals of grammar are part of our mental inheritance makes him very sympathetic to this kind of rationalism. The editor of a recent collection of twelve essays on him notes that "Chomsky has argued from the very beginning that if anything like present-day linguistics is on the right track, then there is a clear sense in which the Rationalists will have been shown to have won out over the Empiricists on the question of the origin of significant components of human knowledge". He adds however, that "that debate is not taken up" by any of the essays in the collection.[20] It seems a pity that Chomsky's fundamental position has remained unchallenged by these dozen learned commentators.

Finally, I need to be explicit about a 'mechanistic' interpretation of behaviour, as such an interpretation may mean different things according to the machine imagined. An animal's capacity to learn distinguishes him from a machine, and it is apropos of this process of adaptation that the 'mechanist' has to face his real problem. If 'mechanistic' means in accord with seventeenth-century ideas of mechanics, then we cannot explain even the working of a steam engine mechanically, much less the behaviour of a rabbit. But if by a mechanistic interpretation we merely mean employing the same principles that we employ in dealing with the behaviour of non-living things, then we must either assume that a mechanistic biology, though possible, is not yet attained, or that science is not one but two. The only argument that can support the latter view is derived from the fact that hitherto the phenomena of life have not been fully interpreted by reference to any principles at all. But the same is true of the phenomena of chemistry and physics, and the real difference of view between investigators depends rather on their hopes and desires. One group hopes that in time all phenomena may be interpreted in terms of one set of principles, while the others hope that some mystery will always remain, so that they may fill up the gap according to taste.

III. The Chimera of Universal Grammar

Linguistic elements are traditionally classified into parts of speech (adjectives, nouns, and so forth) and the sentence into subject, predicate, and other divisions. Grammar is classified into declensions of nouns, conjugations of verbs, agreement, qualification, concordance, and the rest. All such classification is based partly on word forms (mensa, mensam, mensae, and so on) and partly on meaning. The philosophical grammarian finds this double character embarrassing. If we could define a noun as any noise which had a particular kind of meaning, resting the definition exclusively on the meaning, then that would be consistent and logically satisfactory, but from the grammatical and linguistic point of view quite useless. If we could define a noun as a sound having a particular form or subject to a particular kind of alteration, this would be grammatically useful, since the dictionary would need only to indicate the fact that a word is a noun, and we should then be able to deduce all the modifications to which it is subject. This is, in any given language, more or less feasible, but the system which applies in one language is commonly quite useless for another, and so this kind of grammatical analysis is without philosophical interest and concerns only the practical linguist. Between these two the philosophical grammarian is ever seeking a compromise. He wants to preserve his grammatical categories, or at least to substitute something of the same kind, and yet he wants them to have a general validity, not limited to a single language. But what is really common to all languages is only that they can be used to express the same ideas or facts. Hence the philosophical grammarian is always driven back to the *meaning* wherever he looks for a common basis for his universal categories. There is no universal grammar of the slightest interest or value. Generalizations about language are of necessity based on the study of a small selection, and it is fairly safe to say that, the larger the number of languages studied, the fewer the generalizations possible.[21]

Mathematical formulas admit of the substitution of terms on the understanding that all such terms are quantities, differing only in a specific manner. Grammatically identical verbal formulas can seldom be similarly manipulated because their terms are not normally restricted in meaning in some specific way. Grammatically the following sentences are similar, all of the form (A) (B)d a(C):

1. He baked a cake.

2. He smoked a pipe.

3. He wanted an excuse.

4. He purchased a dog.

However, in 1. the cake is the result of a process described by the word 'bake'; in 2. the pipe is a piece of apparatus used for smoking but not in itself appreciably changed in the process; in 3. we have no concrete thing at all, and in 4. it is the relation of dog to owner that is changed. If we consider the meanings of the four verbs and four nouns, there is hardly anything in common in these four propositions, and the relation between the idea expressed by the verb and that expressed by the noun is completely different in each case. Only the grammatical form—pronoun, verb, article, noun—is alike. If logical form means anything else than grammatical form, and if it is supposed to be the same in these four sentences, then it is hard indeed to see in what it consists.

If we are to construct any formula of this kind that will allow a variation of the terms and yet retain some meaning that is unaffected by changing them, we shall have to restrict their meaning considerably. Thus 'he baked a cake' can be changed to 'he made a pudding' or 'he mixed a cocktail'. In each case the grammatical object of the verb expresses the *result* of some activity, and so there is a common framework of meaning which connects these sentences and which might permit us to say that they are variations of one formula; but that common framework involves much more than the grammatical form: subject—verb—object.[22]

In grammar books we frequently meet with rules which are said to apply to verbs having a certain meaning—for instance, verbs of wishing, fearing, or commanding—and formulas are constructed which are valid only for them. If rules of this kind are comparatively few, it is because in the main language consists of words which differ in meaning too much. There exists no systematic classification of words that correspond to any intelligible classification of the parts or aspects of the universe which it has been found convenient to name. As there is an unlimited number of real relations which we may have occasion to express, it would be as useless as it would be impossible to have special grammatical peculiarities for each. When the meaning of verb and noun is known, the relation between them is usually obvious, at all events in a given context. When it is said that 'the mouse gnaws a hole in the floor', it is unnecessary to have any special means (such as formula, suffix, or inflection) of indicating the relationship between 'mouse' and 'gnawing', 'gnawing' and 'hole', 'hole' and 'floor'. If some such verbal indication were provided, how many other cases would there be in which it would be required? Shall we put the gnawing of the mouse into the same class as the sucking of the leech, the chewing of the cow, the scratching of the rabbit, the biting of the carnivore? Shall we take the penetration of a solid material as the character of the class, or the animal nature of the behaviour; or should we separate the action which aims directly at food from that which merely serves to make a passage? So many different classifications are possible that none can be called more logical than another; and any classification would confer no advantage, only an additional burden on the memory, in having a different *kind* of verb, subject or object, or a special particle or inflection or other device for every *kind* of relationship. If the relationship is not obvious from the meaning of the separate terms and from the context of the communication, it will not be made so by selecting from an immense number of special signs for all the conceivable relations in which any object or action can stand to any other.

Exponents of linguistics, however, feel very uneasy about any reliance on meaning. Lyons asks, in a perplexed tone, "the innocent-looking question 'What is the meaning of *cow?*'... Is there any one property, or set of properties, which distinguishes cows from all other objects for which we have different words?" (p. 401). If we forget that 'cow' is a general term for the female of several different mammals, and assume that he is thinking only of the domestic animal found in British meadows, a competent zoologist would have little difficulty in enumerating the characteristic features by which cows can be distinguished from goats, sheep, dogs, cats, and so forth. But the same could not be said of a great many other things which happen to have a common name. It is quite unrealistic to expect a word to have a precise definition which applies on all occasions and in every context. If, instead of a word with a relatively restricted meaning such as 'cow', we took something less easily defined or described, such as a fly or wasp, it would scarcely be possible to suggest a definition or to enumerate the objects denoted, if we took account of common usage. There are thousands of distinct species which are referred to generally as 'flies' and 'wasps'. To the entomologist, the words have a sufficiently precise meaning to allow him to say, after a brief examination, whether any creature shown to him is either a fly or a wasp. His idea of such a creature is an extensive collection of memories of very different specimens in all kinds of different situations. In normal rational discourse, about real things between intelligent people, it is normally possible to agree about the meaning of a word in any given context. But to find a meaning for the word that is valid for every context is usually out of the question. We all use so many of our words somewhat differently, and although we agree fairly well in the application of a certain number of common words, we differ widely in our use of many and can usually communicate at all successfully only with people similar in training and outlook to ourselves, or about things which are of fairly universal interest. A convention may be established between two or more persons that a certain limited number of words shall be used to convey precise items of information or to give specific instructions for a definite and exactly determined action. But this sort of thing is quite out of the question for the common purposes of normal intercourse.

It is very much to Lyons's purpose that he

insists on a distinction between the "sense" of a word and its "reference":

> By the *sense* of a word we mean its place in a system of relationships which it contracts with other words in the vocabulary. . . . Sense . . . carries with it no presuppositions about the existence of objects and properties outside the vocabulary of the language in question. (p. 427)

He is here drawing on terminology introduced by Ogden and Richards. They call the mental event which happens when someone thinks of something a 'reference'—or, as a concession to the vulgar, a thought. The words someone speaks they call 'symbols', and these are said to symbolize his thoughts. When he thinks, he thinks of something, and this something, whatever it may be, they call a 'referent'.[23] Lyons follows them in using (p. 404) 'referents' to mean the things, processes, and events signified by words, but he does not use their term 'references' to mean, as they do, ideas, as he is afraid of committing himself to anything concerning ideas; so he says that 'reference' is "the relationship which holds between words and the things, events, actions and qualities they 'stand for'" (p. 424) and 'reference', he holds, is not the same as 'sense':

> 'Having the same sense'—or synonymy—is a relation which holds between two lexical items [Lyons's term for 'words'] and not between the 'senses' associated with them in the minds of the speakers. (p. 444)

I suggest, as an illustration, that, while we might say that the word 'camel' has a 'referent' which may be inspected in many zoos, it also, for Lyons, has a 'sense', which may be defined, in his terminology (pp. 73–74), by saying that it is 'syntagmatic' with the words 'It is easier for a —————— to go through the eye of a needle than . . .'. That underlying all this is fear of supposed metaphysical problems arising from uncritical acceptance of the existence of ideas is suggested by the following passage:

> It is one of the cardinal principles of 'structuralism' . . . that every linguistic item has its 'place' in a system and its function, or value, derives from the relations which it contracts with other units in the system. . . . Acceptance of the structural approach in semantics has the advantage that it enables the linguist to avoid commitment on the controversial question of the philosophical and psychological status of 'concepts' or 'ideas'. . . . As far as the empirical investigation of the structure of language is concerned, the sense of a lexical item may be defined to be, not only dependent upon, but identical with, the set of relations which hold between the item in question and other items in the same lexical system. (p. 443)

All this over-emphasis on grammar is by no means new. Quite apart from the seventeenth-century grammarians of the Port-Royal, James Mill's whole treatment of abstraction in Chapter 9 of his *Analysis of the Phenomena of the Human Mind* is based on grammar and on the formation of words in the languages he happened to have learned, as if verbal exigencies underlie the whole process. In Chapter 11 he does speak of the "rude and unskilful manner in which naming has been performed",[24] and one might have thought that a realization of this would have warned him of taking the facts of language as his guide. But it is easier to deal with the more or less concrete and accessible facts of language than with non-linguistic processes of the mind.

IV. Conclusion: Language and Thought

The effectiveness of thought does not depend on anything remotely analogous to syntax, but on its derivation from accurate observation and its correspondence with the natural sequence of real events. When I have a real object in my hand, I can examine it and elaborate my idea of it. If I do not have the object available and yet wish to speak of it, I must rely on my memory, my idea; and if I then attempt to describe it, I can only describe my idea. I may, in my imagination, manipulate it and describe the effects of my manipulation, and a great deal of serious thinking consists of mental experimentation of this kind. Cautious thinkers try to confirm their conclusions from mental experiments by experimenting on the real object. Neither physical nor mental experimentation depends on the use of language. Thought can be independent of language, just as speech can be independent of thought, although many writers seem unaware of the extent of either independence. Children can act intelligently before they learn to speak, and they can make vocal sounds before they attach any meaning to them.

In so far as real events may be adequately represented by language, such language can be represented in thought and so serve indirectly to represent the real events. The rules of grammar and syntax are part of the conventions of language and thus contribute to the representational function of language. Their relation to meaning is, however, far from consistent, and the few grammatical rules contained in grammar books bear no comparison with the variety of relations which we are aware of between real things and events. Lyons claims that "the grammatical structure of a language and its semantic structure tend to be highly"—he admits "not totally"—"congruent with one another" (p. 135). If by 'semantic structure' he means the ideas which the language serves to express, then there can be no congruence between language and meaning; for the idea, unless it is a purely verbal one, can never be expressed adequately in words. If it is something more than a mere word, it is not a static entity that can be represented at all adequately by any fixed symbol, whether in sound or picture. In trying to put our ideas into words, we must abridge and select drastically, and rely on our hearer, from his knowledge of us or of our common situation, to reconstruct ideas similar to ours.

Current exaggeration of the role of language in thinking has given exponents of linguistics their opportunity. If logical thinking depends on logical talking, it is clearly important to analyze language. The study of logic has always in practice been closely linked to the study of grammar. Who is better qualified, therefore, to deal with logic and thought than those who are specialists in grammar?

If we wish to understand human reasoning, we need to study the thinking process in other mammals. The biologist is accustomed to look in the less highly developed animal for the rudiments from which the superior faculties of the more highly developed one were derived. Köhler shows very clearly that the mental faculties of man are not fundamentally different from those of the ape. His experiments reveal the part played by reflection in the way chimpanzees solve problems, and his truly masterly descriptions of their behaviour are now achieving adequate recognition.[25] One can argue that a small improvement in the mental capacity of these animals, combined with that physical inferiority which compelled men to organize themselves in society or perish, will have given the conditions for the invention of language. Merely as a means of expression, without specific address, language cannot be supposed to have developed beyond what is found in other animals. It has grown up as a means of communication, and this was required by the complementary relationship between the behaviour of two or more individuals in the co-operation characteristic of a human social group. The multiplication of signs and their organization into a system will not occur unless there is a need, and such need can arise only in a *community*. It is in *co-operating* for a given purpose, in sharing a task, that the attention of one individual can be concentrated at the same time on what he is doing himself and what his companion is doing, since his own action must be accommodated to that of his helper. This interest in the actions of his fellow will tend to stimulate in him the wish to interfere, to correct and guide, and by whatever means he attempts to do this, there is already the beginning of language.

Once it is conceded that human language is an invention, the problem of accounting for it is simplified, or at least becomes part of the larger problem of man's inventiveness. It is then the psychological principles of invention that we have to consult, not grammatical and syntactical features. Man, in his behaviour, differs from the apes chiefly in his inventive capacity. One could say, in the kind of formulation Chomsky uses concerning language, that invention is a uniquely human phenomenon without significant analogue in the animal world. It is true that dogs and cats, and still more apes, do *discover* methods of gaining their ends, and so exhibit a rudimentary power of invention; but the difference between human communication and animal communication is not greater than the difference between human invention in general and animal invention.

The early arguments against the view that language is an invention were based on the assumption that people must have had a language before they could discuss with one another the problem of inventing one; and if language was not invented, it must surely be innate. The obvious answer to this is that the first linguistic signs were not intended to be signs, but were natural reactions to a situation, as when a threatening gesture, such as a shaken fist, is displayed to an intruder. The next stage would have been that, once it had been observed that such a gesture resulted in the intruder withdrawing, it would come to be made *in order* to make him withdraw. In this way a primitive language of self-explanatory signs—gestures and pantomime bearing an obvious relation to meaning—could arise. The wrinkled brow or the smile may be the reflex expression of emotion, in which case they are not gestures. But if they are put on deliberately in order to influence the behaviour of others, then they become gestures. Such natural (universally intelligible) signs must have preceded conventional ones (signs agreed upon among the members of a more or less restricted community).

Generally intelligible signs include pictures or models and dramatic representations as well as gestures, and even a few sounds. Gestures, to be at all explicit, must be developed into dramatic representation of the action required from the person addressed, or of the situation of which one desires to inform him. Although one may represent actions such as chopping or digging without any tool in the hands, it is easier to show one's meaning if one has some object that vaguely resembles the tool; and the more the action depends on the peculiar properties of the objects associated with it, the more necessary will it be to have some material to represent these objects so as to make the gesture clearer. On this basis, we may expect not only pantomime, but also clay models and constructions out of all kinds of handy materials.

For a long time, every possible means must have been employed, each supplementing the other. Constant use of signs of all kinds would lead to their abridgement until they become conventional, in that they were unintelligible to outsiders who had not used them from the first in their unabridged form. At that stage, it will have been discovered that no bond of association between sign and meaning except that of habit is necessary, and that any arbitrary movement, object, noise, or expression may serve as a sign if only the communicating parties recognize the convention. In this way the idea of using deliberately invented conventional signs could arise, and if the signs are to be conventional, they may as well be sounds, which do not immobilize the hands and have other obvious advantages over gestures. Language could then become what it is today—a collection of noises arbitrarily linked to ideas, things, and events.

Chomsky, however, insists on an unbridgeable gap between gesture-language and oral language. It is "quite possible", he says, "that human gestures . . . have evolved from animal communication systems, but not human language. It has a totally different principle". This view is based on gross underestimation of animals' capacity for thinking, for he says on the same page that only man (or his immediate ancestors) can "go beyond just reacting to stimuli". The human "language faculty", he says, has the unique property of "discrete infinity", in that "each sentence has a fixed number of words" and "there is no limit in principle to how many words the sentence can contain", whereas ape calls are limited to "a fixed number, say forty". He thinks it possible that man's ability to construct an infinite series of numbers—"the series goes on indefinitely", "you can always add one more"—is a by-product of the language faculty. Hence he conjectures that, some hundreds of thousands of years ago, perhaps "some mutation took place in the cells of prehuman organisms" which

> led to the representation in the mind/brain of the mechanisms of discrete infinity, the basic concept of language and also of the number system. That made it possible to think, in our sense of thinking. So now humans—or prehumans—could go beyond just reacting to stimuli and could construct complex structures out of the world of their experience, and now, the world of their

imagination. Perhaps that was the origin of human language.[26]

It is really not hard to bridge the gap that prompted this vain theorizing, to see why in time conventional signs supplanted self-explanatory ones. Descriptive signs that do not require knowledge of any conventions are possible only for a limited number of objects and actions. Where they appear to be used for more complex or abstract ideas, there is always a measure of convention. As an illustration, we can and do sometimes name our friends by some descriptive epithet: we observe some peculiarity of bodily form or manner and find some expression that points to it; and names thus assigned could often be directly translated into descriptive or imitative gesture language. But it is only in a small number of cases that such names could be given. To find a descriptive way of indicating every individual would be impossible, unless the descriptive method were extremely complex and comprehensive. On the other hand, every human being can be represented by a name or number, if the connection is allowed to be perfectly arbitrary. Every house can be identified by an address of purely arbitrary names and numbers, but to indicate a particular house without conventional signs so as to distinguish it from all others would often be difficult. We may say, then, that it is only by means of conventional signs that we can find enough distinct signs even for the comparatively small number of things the ordinary person wants to converse about. It is not that conventional signs are better than natural ones, but that one cannot possibly get enough signs without them. However, oral signs, whether conventional or not—although few such signs can be self-explanatory—have enormous advantages due to the manner of producing them and their one-dimensional character.

Sounds must of course have been in use for other purposes before they could be adapted for use in communication: man had to develop the materials of language before he could make use of them for linguistic purposes, as I have already indicated apropos of gestures. Jespersen's conjecture may well be correct, that man originally made sounds merely as a form of play—as activity which "had no other purpose than that of exercising the muscles of the mouth and throat and of amusing oneself and others by the production of pleasant or possibly only strange sounds". Play, performed in times of emotional calm yet of overflowing activity, is certainly conducive to discovery, as the behaviour is less restricted than it is under the pressure of some specific need.

Jespersen declines to say how the transition was made to using sounds as communication: "Association of sound with sense must have been arrived at by devious and circuitous ways which to a great extent evade inquiry and make a detailed exposition impossible".[27] Of course, nobody will expect the details to be made available now, but the general process should be capable of explanation; that is, we ought to be able to say, in general terms, how sound became associated with sense, without being expected to say exactly what sense became attached to what sound. We do not need to suppose that the whole process of constructing a language consisted in the gradual acquisition of meaning by sounds uttered in play. It seems absurd to exclude conscious effort from this one invention when we take it for granted in every other. Of course there is always the lucky discovery, but the progress of invention is to be ascribed not so much to these lucky chances as to the readiness to appreciate their significance and exploit the discovery. The fact that noises could be used as signs instead of all the other gestures and representations used for the purpose was a discovery, whether it was made once or often. It could not be made unless the two components already existed, the vocal acts and the use of signs. The former are, I have suggested, correctly explained by Jespersen: they were employed in play as we can see not only among children and uncivilized peoples, but even among dogs. The use of signs is intelligible if one takes gestures as one's point of departure. Other animals use signs. The important human invention consisted rather in the systematic development of this method of communication once the principle had been recognized. I have gone into all this elsewhere,[28] and the view that communication depended initially on gesture and pantomime now commands sizable assent.[29] Nevertheless, many who write on language and on human thinking and behaviour are so anxious to have their work regarded as on a level with what is done in the 'exact' sciences that they look for something recondite and scorn obvious and straightforward explanations which detract from the value of specialist knowledge.

3
Magic and Ritual

The reader may query the relevance of my discussion of the origin of language at the end of the previous chapter, and may ask: does it matter what the ancestral forms of anything were if we know its function today? In the case of animal organs, for instance, can one hope to understand any better the function of the human ear by knowing the evolutionary history of the auditory ossicles? For most purposes—medical, surgical, and psychological—this history is admittedly irrelevant, yet if we did not know it, we might be inclined to look for non-existent functions. When it is asked why an animal should have an organ of this form rather than that, we are inclined to see in such peculiarities an indication of a close relation to the needs of the animal; whereas they may in truth be merely the vestige of an obsolete organ, or the consequence of some ancient transformation. An organ which has been modified so as to serve a new function under different conditions may retain features that have no relation to the new conditions and merely survive as relics of a vanished state of affairs. If an organ has been created for the fulfilment of a specific function, one expects it to be efficient. But if it has merely been adapted from something which previously served a different purpose, then its imperfections are less surprising.

In questions of anatomy, it may be that serious misapprehensions are unlikely to arise in this way, for the organs are tangible and subject to direct experimentation, so that theories of function can be tested in unambiguous ways. But in the case of psychological functions and forms of behaviour, we are in a very different position. Hence to understand language's limitations, we ask about its origin; and to check the mental operations of philosophers, we must be prepared to study the comparative psychology of thought: man is a mammal, with a brain constructed on the same lines as that of other mammals and closely resembling that of an anthropoid ape.

Fundamentally, language, whether it consists of sounds or some other signs, is a form of behaviour adapted for the control of other living beings. It is in order to evoke various desired responses from his human or other companions that a dog indulges in barking, whining, or growling. Just as man's behaviour generally aims at adapting his environment, including his neighbours, to suit his own requirements, so language is a manner of guiding and determining to some extent the behaviour of certain other beings. That this, the imposition of will rather than the exchange of ideas, was the primary function of language is suggested by its magical uses.

As an example which typifies magical practices, the relevant article in a standard religious encyclopaedia mentions the custom, in a certain part of southern Africa, of attracting rain by dipping branches of trees in water and then swinging them through the air so as to make the drops fall from them. As further instances of such "imitative" magic, the author of this article gives: blowing tobacco smoke or feathers into the air to attract clouds, and jumping high in dances, or dancing on stilts, so as to make crops grow tall. In all these instances, he says, there is no question of addressing and trying to influence some deity: the procedure is quite impersonal and based on the conviction that it will itself automatically produce the required result. He thinks that the origin of such practices is too obscure ever to be fully explained.[1]

Frazer's ideas on the psychology of magic are now justly rejected. He supposed magical practices to be based on two convictions: 1. that things which resemble each other are the same; and 2. that things which had once been in contact with each other are always in contact. Thus 1. sprinkling water in order to produce rain implies the delusion that the water sprinkled is the rain desired; and 2. operations performed on a severed lock of hair are believed to affect the owner of the hair because the two were once in contact. Commentators rightly say, with Beattie, that "nobody in their senses" could possibly believe such things, and that tribes which based their behaviour on Frazer's two principles could not have survived.[2]

The reaction against Frazer has led many to deny that magical rites are intended to produce any practical results at all, and to claim that they amount to no more than an expression of wishes. On this view, the man who makes magic over the plants in his garden is simply expressing the wish that they will grow and does not suppose that his magic will actually promote their growth. Hostility to Frazer has gone so far as to include what has been called "a general criticism of the entire assumption that people's actions can be explained by their beliefs".[3] Wittgenstein, for instance, held that primitive man does not "act from opinions", and that primitive magic is akin to kissing the portrait of a beloved one—an action which is an expression of emotion, and certainly not intended to have some effect on the beloved person.[4] Beattie, however, believes—surely correctly—that magic, although expressive, is also thought to be efficacious (or "instrumental" in his terminology). He says, taking verbal magic as his example, that

> Many people think that the word, the *logos,* has its own special power. Often it is believed that to say or even to think something solemnly and emphatically enough is somehow to make it more likely to happen. Even members of modern societies may be frightened and ashamed when they become conscious of hidden wishes for the death or injury of someone they dislike, and many feel guilt when the object of their antipathy is run over by a bus. Belief in the power of words, thoughts and symbols is by no means a monopoly of simpler peoples. (p. 204)

Phillips says, in a similar vein:

> I may express the wish that someone should come to me by beckoning or calling out to him. When he comes, I may feel that this is due to some inherent power in the beckoning or calling: almost as if a power accompanies the gesture or words.[5]

In fact, of course, the power of gestures or words is due to their being understood by an intelligent (animal or human) respondent. But if even today there can be a residual feeling that their efficacy is not restricted in this way, does this not suggest that, in primitive conditions, this restriction was not appreciated at all, and that they were believed to produce their effects of themselves? I stress that I am here concerned with the *origin* of magical practices. Some who perform them today may well regard them as no more than expressive. But they are too widespread and too important among uncivilized peoples to have arisen in this way.

The reader will probably object that it is not easy to see how, once any form of communication had been invented, the devices used in effecting it (gestures, words, etc.) should be so grossly misunderstood. But although men had invented language, they surely did not all, in its early days, understand why it worked, because, as always, there are those who invent and those—the great majority—who can only use the inventions without understanding more than is necessary for some practical applications of them. Englefield has pointed to the fact that examples of belief in the magical properties of a later form of communication, namely writing, amply demonstrate the possibility of such misunderstandings, by analogy with which earlier forms (necessarily prehistoric) can be reconstructed.[6]

There are in fact many stories of persons who knew nothing about writing being astonished to observe how mysterious marks on paper could convey an influence from their author to a distant stranger. Since the marks are meaningless to the uninitiated person, he is ready to attribute the same power to other unfamiliar markings, and also to assume that the power in question is much wider than it in fact is. Those who wrote charms might attribute more weight to the formula itself, to the meaning of the words it contains; for they could distinguish between the correctly and the incorrectly written formula. But for the illiterate this distinction did not exist. The symbols were unintelligible, therefore mysterious, and therefore probably potent.

Faith in the magical power of written spells will not, then, have originated among persons familiar with the art of reading and writing, but among those who are aware of the existence of writing, who observe its practice by certain gifted individuals, who realize that it gives them inexplicable powers, but who do not understand at all the principles on which it depends. But while written charms can exist only among peoples who have made some acquaintance with writing, verbal magic, resting on the imaginary powers of spoken words, is found everywhere, and it is more difficult to see how people could remain unaware of the nature and limits of the virtue of words. In view, however, of the widespread mysticism associated with the study of language in historical times, we are justified in supposing that the communities in which the art originated had a very imperfect understanding of its nature. If, as is now widely agreed, language began with gesture and pantomime, then, as Englefield observes:

> There was surely once a time when conventional oral languages were a novelty and used only by initiates; magical beliefs about the

power of these bizarre utterances having once originated could continue to be attached to special languages and formulas after a vulgar language had become widespread.[7]

By uttering a man's name, one could summon him. By saying 'strangle Tom', one in authority might in fact accomplish Tom's undoing; and for those who did not share the secrets of language, the process by which the result was brought about would be mysterious. That the use of the name did in fact sometimes give some degree of control over the owner of the name, whether man or animal, was a matter of perfectly correct observation. What the observation could not supply was information concerning the extent of such control. It is thus possible that, from the observed potency of words, there should result the belief that, by uttering the right words, one might bring about any desired results. As the use of language became more widespread and vulgarized, and the real limits of its efficacy determined by experience, verbal magic became restricted to archaic or unintelligible formulas handed down from ancient times, or formulas which possessed some extraneous sanctity through their author or origin.[8]

In sum, the magical efficacy of verbal formulas is to be traced to a genuine recognition of the power of words, combined with a failure to appreciate the true nature of that power and its limitations. Le Dantec says:

> It is certainly through the medium of words that men exchange ideas. It is through words that a chief commands his subjects. But from the fact that certain conventional phonetic

signs, transmitted among families and by education, are used for communication between men of the same country, people have come to attribute, *with no logic at all,* a universal importance to these words, which really are effective only between one person and another. People have come to believe that these words command the elements. They have deified the verb (Italics added).[9]

But not 'with no logic at all'. The logic may have been imperfect and the fallacy easy now to detect, but a generalization is not illogical. Man invented the potent engine of language, but how could he understand its powers? In some respects it was destined to accomplish for him things of which he could not dream; in others it fell short of his too sanguine hopes. Only time and experience could reveal these things.

As already noted, a good deal of magic is gestural rather than verbal. Frazer, describing the practices of the rain makers of the Upper Nile, says that, among other things, they take a cane in their hands and beckon with it to the clouds to come, or wave them away in the direction they should go. It is recorded of the natives of the Loyalty Islands in the South Pacific that, on sighting a shoal of porpoises, they go out in a canoe to where they are, and by means of "vehement gestures and persuasive native oratory", persuade these "fish" to follow the canoe, which is gently paddled towards the shore.[10] This is a remarkable instance of magic in the making: the application of methods in use for controlling human beings to the purpose of controlling sea mammals.

Gestures provide only limited possibilities for suggesting ideas. They can represent an action by actually performing it, and an object by tracing its outline in the air or on the ground, or by showing it, or some part of it, or something associated with it. Pictorial methods can supplement this by making an actual drawing or model of it. Budge gives examples in his *Egyptian Magic* of pictures being placed with the dead to ensure the supply to the latter of the articles represented by the pictures. He also instances making a model of a person or object that it is desired to injure or affect in any way, and then destroying or mutilating it. A sorcerer who wishes to kill someone may make a wax figure of the victim and then melt it in the fire or impale it with pins. The relation between such practices and pictorial methods of communication is fairly obvious, and the construction of an image, or the drawing of a picture, must have been one of the earliest and most natural forms of pre-vocal communication. To produce in the mind of an audience the idea of some person or object, what better than to present some representation of him or it? And the idea of inflicting injuries on someone can be evoked by the gesture of injuring his effigy. This idea, once evoked, could be put into practice, so that the indirect effects of awakening such an idea may be very conspicuous, and so may, by some observers, come to be attributed to the image or model itself.

Lord Avebury (John Lubbock) quotes a passage from Plutarch which expressly links magical pantomime with the gesture language used in communication:

> The traveller who has little or no acquaintance with the language of the land in which he is resorts naturally to the language of

gesture, and mimics the thing which he wishes to have done. Primitive man communicates his wishes to Nature in exactly the same way: if he wishes to have game caught in the trap which he sets, he first pretends to fall into it himself.[11]

If I want someone, in a given situation, to climb a wall or a hill, I could convey the idea to him by jumping, and then pointing to the wall. Hence we may suppose that, when natives jump in their ritual dances to make their crops grow high, this practice originated as an attempt to influence the crops themselves by the same means as were once employed to influence fellow beings. The same is true of sprinkling water to attract rain, roaring to encourage thunder, and whistling for the wind. It is really quite unsatisfactory to explain such practices by saying that they "seem to stem from instinctive miming of what is profoundly desired."[12] To assume such an instinct is gratuitous. I find Englefield's argument much more convincing: namely that the inference on which these methods originally rested was that, since such signs were effective when employed on fellow human beings, they might usefully be tried on other things.

It may be that gestures were employed instead of speech because it was supposed that spirits were being addressed, that the idea was not to influence crops and other natural phenomena directly, but the powers behind the scenes, who had to be addressed in a *lingua franca,* just as did foreigners who spoke a different tongue. But we are not obliged to assume that the purely psychological effectiveness of gesture or other language was understood from the first. The consciousness that these methods of control produced results may well have preceded any clear notion as to how. Quite possibly this was the original situation, but as the methods of communication became more familiar and their limitations were revealed by practical experience, the view that spirits were being addressed would begin to predominate, being partly determined by the desire to explain the magical practices prescribed by tradition. At this stage, then, many magical forms will have tended to resume their original function and were used as a mode of communication, this time with the deities. This communication could be imperative in intent. As I have noted, by speaking a man's name, one could summon him; and "if power can be exerted over men by the use of their names, it is only reasonable to believe that spirits and deities can be similarly influenced."[13]

Words and pantomime are often combined. Tambiah notes that, in most Zande rites, "the wished-for effect is stated *verbally* simultaneously with or before the carrying out of the so-called 'homeopathic' act (of influencing certain objects by manipulating other objects which resemble them)". For instance, to make the oil-bearing melon flourish, the natives use the tall *bingba* grass, which is profuse in growth and has feather-like branches; and they use it both "by verbal direction and by direct action".[14] Now combining different methods—verbal and pictorial among others—must have been characteristic of early communication. If one could not convey a certain idea by words alone, then added pantomime might do the trick. To convey the idea of rampant growth, or to convey an instruction that one's subordinates should set to work (in ways which they knew and which therefore needed no mention) to make the crops flourish, one could display an object which was known to be profuse in growth, as well as trying to suggest the idea or the instruction in words. Does this not suggest (although Tambiah does not draw this inference) that the corresponding magical practice arose through misapplication of this practical form of behaviour? Tambiah adds:

> In a laboratory today, the only time a scientist may be found to foretell and verbally explain his actions while simultaneously doing his experiment would be, for example, when he is teaching a class the procedure involved in conducting the experiment.[15]

That is, in a situation where he is communicating practical instructions.

If we turn now from individual practices to communal ritual, some of its forms may well have originated as dramatic magic, as methods of controlling human enemies or nature—bringing back the rain, fertilizing the ground. The ritual will have consisted in dramatic performances which were supposed to effect these ends. There is evidence that some peoples, before going on the warpath or the chase, perform a mimetic dance in which the foe or the quarry are represented as falling before their weapons. Before oral language was available, that is, when communication had to be effected by gesture or pantomime, such ritual would have served the purposes of announcing to the community that a war or a hunt was about to be undertaken, and of enhancing the courage of the potential warriors and huntsmen through the excitement that accompanied the performance. In time, such representative dances or actions that originally owed their effectiveness to this communicative value, could come to be used—after oral language had made them unnecessary—with purely magical intent.

As for bringing back the life-giving rains and fertilizing the seeds, we may note that one obvious way of conveying by gesture the idea of 'life' or 'alive' to another person would be to throw oneself on the ground, simulating death, and then spring up again, with an expression of triumph, indicating a condition opposite to that of death. Englefield asks, apropos of such pantomime:

> When the seed is put into the ground it appears to die, and out of the dead body there seems to spring the new plant. 'That which thou sowest is not quickened except it die'. Paul saw in this a parallel to the resurrection. Can we not suppose that the same parallel had previously given rise to the magical process of pretending to raise a human being from the dead in order to produce a good harvest by encouraging the young plants to grow out of the dead seed?[16]

Originally there was probably no idea of addressing a god; the action was believed to bring about its effects automatically. But we do not have to suppose that there existed the same clear idea of the difference between the two processes that we have now. It was because the true nature of the effect of communicative gestures was not understood that they were used in circumstances where they were necessarily ineffectual. But in time the performance came to be maintained by tradition, its origin being forgotten; and especially when other forms of communication were universally adopted, the use of pantomime as a normal mode of communication would have been lost.

There was always room for a certain amount of hocus-pocus or make-believe in the organization of these ritual observances; for the organizers— medicine men or chiefs—will have exercised a good deal of control over the ceremonies, and will have introduced or exaggerated some features for the sake of making a deeper impression on naive onlookers, rather than for enhancing the effectiveness of the magic. Nevertheless, magic as a whole, whether communal or private, cannot be regarded as a mere conspiracy of witches and wizards. The force of suggestion may enable us to understand how faith in magical practices was perpetuated, but it does not explain how the particular kinds of practice which we find to be almost universal came to be adopted. Suggestion could but confirm the efficacy of any practice to which faith had once been attached. It is notorious that loopholes were provided to account for failures (explained, for instance, as due to the force of countervailing magic). But these loopholes were not necessarily conscious safeguards. Where faith is strong, rationalization is easy. Convinced Freudians or Marxists have little difficulty in explaining away failures in their theories.

When the community is a populous city it ceases to have the same interest in the harvest. Food is bought, not produced. It must of course be produced somewhere, but the urban population is much less conscious of the whole agricultural process. If the fertility ritual survives in these urban conditions, it will be reinterpreted. One may suppose that originally, in order to ensure the return of summer, a magical performance was instituted in which the death and resurrection of the season was suggested by the death and resurrection of a man or animal. This was a magical proceeding based on dramatic communication. At a later date, this rite, no longer understood as magical, may well have been explained as commemorative: the man represented some personage who at some time in the past had died and then come to life again. This explanation consists in a narrative of events, and this narrative can in time be elaborated. In this way, myths could arise explaining a form of ritual the origin of which is forgotten. The later theory that the adventures of gods who died and came to life again were symbolical representations of natural phenomena perhaps arose because the dramatic rituals were in fact originally performed in order to bring about certain desired phenomena. Thus myths about these gods might be taken to be an anthropomorphic interpretation of the changing seasons.

One possibility is that the ritual becomes more elaborate, spectacular, and expensive. The religious significance might then become almost secondary, entertainment predominating. The old elements—singing, dancing, drama—would be performed by professionals and the majority of the participants would be merely spectators. On the other hand, for that section of the community which was depressed and deprived of all prosperity, the ritual could become a means of ensuring a better deal in another world: the spectacle of the god's conquest of death could be taken by them as an assurance of their own blessed immortality. In this way, we can understand the development of the mystery religions.[17] Thus, out of the primitive ritual designed to promote the fertility of the land by magical means, there could grow on the one hand modern forms of entertainment, and on the other new forms of religion.

That myths are no more than attempts—naive and sincere, or sophisticated and fraudulent—to explain, by means of a narrative in historical terms, a rite, custom, belief, or indeed anything else, is not today a popular view. Malinowski initiated the reaction against it when he wrote:

> Studied alive, myth, as we shall see, is not symbolic, but a direct expression of its subject-matter; it is not an explanation in satisfaction of a scientific interest, but a narrative resurrection of a primitive reality, told in satisfaction of deep religious wants, moral cravings, social submissions, assertions, even practical requirements. Myth fulfils in primitive culture an indispensable function: it expresses, enhances, and codifies belief; it safeguards and enforces morality; it vouches for the efficiency of ritual and contains practical rules for the guidance of man. Myth is thus a vital ingredient of human civilization; it is not an idle tale, but a hard-worked active force; it is not an intellectual explanation or an artistic imagery [sic], but a pragmatic character of primitive faith and moral wisdom.[18]

This rhetorical exercise conveys only that this thing called myth is highly respectable, has been much maligned by previous anthropologists, and can be restored to its proper dignity by field workers, such as the writer himself, who have studied it "alive" instead of in books like other people. This innuendo that only field workers have any right to pronounce on the subject is on the same level as the claim, still sometimes made, that all worthwhile historiography entails direct study of original documents. In fact, however, one has to trust scholarly editions of famous texts, estimating in each particular case what amount of possible error must be allowed for. One cannot repeat all the enquiries and comparisons of manuscripts underlying a text prepared by a respectable professor who has no other task in life but to perform such work. If a historian cannot trust the printed editions of other scholars, but must study every manuscript for himself, then he will produce nothing.

Religious apologists have responded to Malinowski with gratitude. If they cannot deny that their sacred books include a great deal of myth, they can nevertheless claim—as does John Robinson in his *Honest to God*—that myth is "an important form of religious truth".[19]

The view of magic I have argued in this chapter is also not what recent writers on the subject would accept. Many of them, as we saw, so far from trying to explain why futile magical practices are resorted to in order to achieve practical ends, have denied that magicians envisage practical effects at all—although what they are supposed to be envisaging is often not made at all clear. For instance, Geertz, who thinks that Indians who throw water up into the air "in an imitative sort of way" in their rain dance are not thereby trying to produce rain, is impressed by Susanne Langer's thesis that they are "trying to think about the way in which the various parts of the cosmos as they conceive it, explicitly or implicitly, connect up with each other."[20] But this is make-believe, not explanation. G.E.R. Lloyd is at least intelligible when he declares that "magic, so it has been forcefully and in part, at least, surely rightly argued, should be seen less as attempting to be efficacious than as affective, expressive or symbolic". He adds: "The criteria that are relevant to judging magical behaviour are not whether it achieves practical results, but whether it has been carried out appropriately or not".[21] The belief that faithful adherence to all the details prescribed by tradition is important is not hard to explain, and certainly does not mean that practical results are not looked for. If one's actions aim at building a canoe or felling a tree, the effect of each action (as appropriate or not to the aim) can be seen at once, and the behaviour modified so that it is optimally adapted to achieving the aim. If however the aim is to cure an illness or make crops grow by various ritual actions, the connection between these and the result is not at all obvious, and the safest course is therefore to perform the whole series of actions which have habitually been performed for this purpose in the past. In this case, the precise effect of omitting or varying something cannot be ascertained, and so it is best to keep to the time-honoured routine.

There is nothing specifically religious in reliance on routine. Once a series of actions aiming at an immediate practical result has been found to work, they are performed without reflection, as when we learn in time to put on our clothes and clean our teeth. A good deal of more complicated behaviour, which in our youth involved us in *moral* choice, also becomes routine as we grow older. The characteristic of magic rituals, and of religious rituals generally, is that *ineffectual* practices have become stereotyped—not in consequence of success in achieving the aim, but as a consequence of ignorance as to how the behaviour and the aim are really connected.

In defence of the view that magic is intended to be efficacious, it has repeatedly been pointed out that it is most commonly resorted to apropos of such matters of crucial importance to the individuals or communities concerned as are not within their power to control by ordinary means, illness and weather being the two most obvious examples. It has also been observed that practitioners feel the need to offer some explanation when results are not produced, for instance by attributing failure to countervailing sorcery on the part of someone else, or to negligence over some detail of the necessary rites.[22]

A further factor is that to view magic as the extending of a valid correlation or generalization beyond its proper confines enables us to see it as an example of a very common and understandable source of error. Belief in the elixir of life, for instance, obviously arose by generalizing too widely. So many ailments yielded to the prescriptions of the wise man, why not eventually all? So many causes of death may be circumvented and resisted, why not all? Because certain medicines have an unmistakable effect on the body, why should there not exist a physic, if only it could be found, for every possible ill? Palmistry and phrenology can be explained as of similar origin. It was observed that character and bodily form are not entirely unconnected, and that fortune was in a measure dependent on character. It was then inferred that the correlation between fortune and bodily form was complete, and that to discover the former it was necessary only to study the minute details of the latter. That the lines of the hand and the bumps on the head were selected as of special importance was due to the fact that they offered a promising variety of data, and perhaps also to the fact that hand and head were recognized as the most important human members.

Astrology can likewise be understood as untoward extension of a valid generalization. Although astrology is sometimes held to have preceded astronomy, this can be true only if by astronomy is meant the modern science. Some more or less accurate observations of the movements of celestial bodies must have been made before it was possible to attribute any significance at all, however fanciful, to such movements. Volney noted in 1791 that, before the invention of a calendar, agriculturalists could know only from the stars when it was time to sow or harvest. Having thus observed that these activities bore a regular and constant connection with the stars, it was easy to infer influence from correlation, and also to suppose that this influence extended to other human affairs. If the stars can inform me that farmer Jones will soon be using his plough, perhaps closer scrutiny of them may reveal that he will shortly fall sick or inherit money.[23]

The extending of a real correlation or generalization beyond the limits of its true validity is of a piece with scientific errors, as we saw apropos of the Pythagorians (above, p. 60). Indeed, Pavlov's experiments have shown that mammals other than man generalize too readily, and that a first rough and approximate generalization, which has later to be refined and restricted in its scope is of great importance for learning.[24] To explain the origin of magic practices in terms of premature generalization has, then, the merit of bringing them into line with much in human, indeed in mammalian behaviour generally.

The importance of the process of generalization for thinking is today often underestimated because of emphasis on the role of hypothesis—as if the two were alternatives. In actual fact, hypothesis is very much involved in the reaching of generalizations, as can be illustrated from the familiar case of theories about the heavenly bodies. The first serious attempts to explain their motion were based on the hypothesis of a primeval chaos from which gradually the different parts sorted themselves out, with the earth as the centre and the sun and moon, separated from it, travelling round it. Careful observation of the motions of the planets and the phases of the moon led in time to the hypothesis that the moon circled the earth, and the earth and the other planets circled the sun. This hypothesis explained the changing position of the planets (the wandering stars) and also the phases of the moon, with the assistance of the further assumption that the earth revolved on its axis. Such explanations were acceptable because they appealed to common facts of experience. All explanation must be in terms of what is familiar or accepted, and people were familiar with the fact that objects do travel through space and that the illumination of a revolving spherical ball by a single source of light affects only one hemisphere at a time. One residual perplexity was the perpetual motion of the heavenly bodies, as this kind of motion did not occur in the experience of man on earth: objects could be projected through space for a considerable distance, but they always came to the ground again. It was also contrary to common experience that the earth should be a sphere, since one would expect things to fall off the lower half: experience offered only rare examples of mutual attraction between particles of matter. A more exact study of the velocities of falling objects led to the hypothesis of universal gravitation, so that the final explanation of the apparent motions of sun and moon consisted in a simple generalization concerning the motions of bodies in space. If it were asked *why* objects moved according to this 'law', the only possible answer would consist in a yet wider generalization.

What, then, is the rôle of the hypothesis? The moon appears to us, when it is full, like a circular white disc. We make the hypothesis that it is a spherical mass, and ask: if it were of such a size and at such a distance, would it appear to us as it does? If yes, then this is so far a plausible hypothesis. The phases of the moon led to the further hypothesis that it is not a luminous body, but is illuminated by the sun, and the hypothesis of a spherical body fits in with this. It amounts to this: having established a law, we must decide whether every particular case, every particular application falls under it or not, and we often have to make the hypothesis so as to bring the phenomenon under the law. Having done so, we test our hypothesis by asking whether it fits other laws, in so far as they have any application. And so, in the end, a scientific explanation of anything consists in showing that it is a particular case of a general law.

I am not suggesting that every magical practice can be directly traced to a process of premature generalization, or indeed to any effective form of behaviour. Once established, magical practices would suggest others, and origins will have been quickly lost from sight, even if they had ever been properly understood. Magical ceremonies as we actually find them practised are survivals. They can no more be explained in terms of the general conceptions of those who practise them than many modern European superstitions can be explained in terms of modern ideas. And, like modern religious rites, they must be regarded as compounded of different elements of different antiquity. Ceremonies are persisted in even when those who perform them are quite unaware of the reasons which led to their institution. The grounds on which in the first place a ceremony was introduced may even be contemptuously rejected by those who, in ignorance of them, continue to perform the ceremony.[25]

It is perhaps appreciation of such factors as these that is responsible for a widespread tendency today to belittle the influence of reasoned beliefs on behaviour and to stress the role of emotion (as when magical rites are construed as mere expressions of strong wishes). It is not always appreciated how closely intertwined intellect and emotion are. It would be hard to say what the specific nature of any emotion is apart from the ideas, perceptions, and actions which accompany it, although it can be judged by various means as to its strength. A pure emotion that is not accompanied by some memory, some mental representation of things or events, is perhaps impossible, and could at all events have no definite effect on behaviour, which needs to be related to the present situation and often also to memories of the past. As for intellect, reflection occurs characteristically under the pressure of some emotion, some desire or fear, some impulse toward or away from a certain condition or situation. The natural tendency of any stimulus of interest to the individual is reaction, but reaction may not be possible. In, for instance, a dangerous situation, obvious escape routes may be blocked, and the individual then has to think out an alternative. This process of reflection involves envisaging a wider situation than the one already present, and this means delay, for aspects of this wider situation cannot all be envisaged simultaneously, but must be recalled successively. One may say that the *size* of an idea depends on the number and variety of particular experiences that have contributed to it and can be recalled in support of it. Perhaps, when immediate reaction *is* possible, there is no emotion. Fear is said not to be experienced by the fugitive when in full flight, but only when he seeks to flee and cannot. In the former case, energy is expended in violent action as soon as it is generated, while in the latter the visceral excitement—the secretion of adrenelin, the acceleration of the heart-beat—maintains the individual in a state of tension that he experiences as emotion.

❧ 4
Language and the Bible

I. Biblical Language as 'Polysemous'

One way of avoiding the inconvenience and embarrassment of taking what the Bible says in its plain straightforward sense is to allege that its sense is not plain and straightforward at all. John Tinsley (Bishop of Bristol until 1985) maintains that biblical revelation cannot be rendered in "some prose paraphrase"; it is not "simple" but "subtle" and "many-sided", "indirect rather than direct", and hence "on an altogether higher plane of reality and significance". In particular, "God's manner in Christ" is of this "indirect, elusive, enigmatic" nature.[1]

A generation earlier, Ian Ramsey, Bishop of Durham, was arguing that the language of the Bible is of a special kind, and that "no attempt to make it conform to a precise, straightforward public language—whether that language be scientific or historical—has ever succeeded". In

147 ❧

particular, "the language of the Gospels . . . must be odd enough to be appropriate to the odd situations which are their subject".[2] The implication is that we have a good deal of freedom in saying what such language means. Instead of accepting the old rigid dogmas, "we have to learn the thrill of theological exploration, the delight of theological discovery. . . . It is this we must substitute for a be-all and end-all theology".[3]

On this view, then, language may be either 'public' or 'odd'. Public language is presumably the kind we use when we wish to be understood, whereas odd language has no universally agreed meaning but may be interpreted in a spirit of 'theological discovery'. There does not seem to be any way of distinguishing specimens of the two kinds of language. A given passage may appear to have a clearly intelligible meaning and yet in fact be of the 'odd' variety and mean something else, perhaps even anything else, according to taste, although Ramsey is anxious to avoid such relativism and insists that his doctrine does not imply that "anybody's guess is as good as anyone else's".[4] Obviously, some parts of the Bible are to be understood as statements of historical fact, open, perhaps, to minimal correction, so that, even if we do not believe that Jesus was born at Bethlehem in the reign of Herod the Great, we nevertheless accept that his birth occurred about the Year 1 somewhere in the East. But there is no means of knowing how much of the rest must be given such straightforward interpretation. The statements about his virgin birth and his coming to life after having died on the cross are clearly odd and so are appropriate subjects for 'theological exploration'. But the statements that he had twelve disciples and that one was called Peter and another John should probably be regarded as historical—until someone can show that they are mythical. Then, of course, we shall have to interpret them differently.

Views such as those of Tinsley and Ramsey are commonly defended on the ground that a text may suggest different ideas and emotions to the same person (including its author) in different situations. Since the 1920s, a series of literary critics have supposed that this is particularly true of poetry. I.A. Richards declares:

> The threads of relevant connection which the poem may touch, as it enters into now one, now into another of the vast reservoirs of experience in different minds, are too various, complex and subtle for any external observer to trace. In this sense, there is far more in any poem than one reader can discover.[5]

It is with such doctrine in mind that Dennis Nineham suggests that biblical passages, like poems, have multiple meanings. The meaning a biblical story was designed to convey is, he argues, not its only meaning and is unlikely to be a significant meaning for us today; it is evidence only of "how people of between 2,000 and 3,000 years ago responded to reality". Later ages are unlikely to be able to respond in the same way. For instance, "anyone familiar with the most probable translation and interpretation of the [Lord's] prayer will be aware that comparatively little of it can be used today in its original sense".[6]

This appeal to modern poetic theory is of very questionable value. Most words are apt to excite in the hearer's mind a variety of thoughts and memories if time is allowed for their revival; and a word or phrase does not have any more associations when it occurs in verse than in prose. It may be that, when we come across the word 'golden' in a poem, we shall not expect to find the precious element referred to, as we should if we found the word in a jeweller's catalogue. But this difference can only be due to the fact that, when reading poetry, we adapt ourselves, perhaps unconsciously, to the conventions as known to us. The associations are in our minds, and may or may not be evoked. Further, if when reading either verse or prose we were to linger long enough over every suggestive word in order to discover them, we should read very slowly and lose much of the pleasure. In consequence, many commentators see their function as providing the reader with what they regard as relevant associations so that, without having to read intolerably slowly, he can yet discern a richness and variety of meaning which he would not himself have suspected. The meaning of a word is made up of associations, but we may profitably distinguish between those associations likely to be common between writer and readers—such there must be, otherwise there would be no common language —and those which are peculiar to one reader and may even result only from his protracted reflection. Empson's *Seven Types of Ambiguity,* first published in 1930, typifies the method of those critics who, by a process which seems to be borrowed from the psychoanalysts, explore their own recondite associations and then say that they are in the text on which they are commenting. This is quite absurd. The song of a blackbird likewise excites all sorts of feelings and ideas in different minds or at different times, yet there would be no sense in saying that these are in the song, or that the skylark was the real author of Shelley's poem.

However, the obvious advantage of drawing on free associations when elucidating a text is that the commentator can thereby make it mean whatever suits his prejudice or convenience; and some theologians have been quick to grasp that they can 'actualize' the Bible and make it 'relevant' in this way. In chapter five of Mark's gospel, Jesus cures a woman who had suffered from haemorrhages for twelve years. Glebe-Möller, Professor of Dogmatics at Copenhagen, comments: menstrual bleeding represents sexuality, sexuality is related to violence, and so Jesus's action "seeks to put an end to violence". In this way, Glebe-Möller attains his "alternative Christology", which he needs because he can "no longer think of a God who lets his son die for the sake of humans".[7]

John Polkinghorne is also beholden to the doctrines of modern literary criticism, saying as he does that "symbol, because of its poetic openness of meaning, proves to be the natural language of theology".[8] Polkinghorne was Professor of theoretical physics at Cambridge when he relinquished his Chair to become ordained as an Anglican priest. After two years of parish work, he returned to Cambridge as Dean and Chaplain of Trinity Hall and is now President of Queen's College. "The symbol", he says, "carries a cloud of allusion and suggestion which enables individuals to respond to it in their own way" (p. 31). He allows that some biblical passages are morally offensive if taken in their plain sense: there are "distressing harshnesses in tales of genocide and stoning to death and in the vindictiveness of the cursing psalms" (p. 67). Even the New Testa-

ment, to which, in the manner of Christian commentators, he is noticeably kinder, raises problems because of its "contrasting points of view"
and at times "disturbingly 'mythical' language".
(The inverted commas are meant as protective, as
a signal that 'mythical' is not to be understood
purely negatively.) As an example he mentions
"the notion, so important to Pauline thought, that
there are non-human authorities and powers at
work in the world"—supernatural evil powers
and demons. He does not reject this as supersti-
tion, but thinks it possible to make sense of it by
reference to "Jungian studies of depth psychology", which "seem to indicate that there are
powerful symbols active in the unconscious . . .
whose continuing recurrence in widely different
circumstances suggests that they possess a degree
of autonomy independent of individual men".[9]
Beneath all the perplexities, he claims to discern,
as the Bible's "ground bass and unifying principle", its "continuing testimony to the steadfast
love of God and his Christ". It is in order to make
the reading of Scripture thus "truly edifying" that
we must, in his view, assimilate our study of it to
"our fundamental experience of open engage-
ment with symbol" (p. 67). It would therefore, he
says, be quite wrong to suppose that a particular
passage means only what its author intended—as
wrong as supposing that the meaning of a word is
given by its etymology (p. 68). I find this analogy
quite spurious. The Italian word 'gambetto'
means a small leg, then it comes to be used for a
short stalk, then for the action of tripping. From
this it is transferred to chess, where it is applied to
certain initial moves which involve the sacrifice of
a pawn or piece. Nowadays it is often used for any
beginning or initial step. Etymology is full of

examples of such transfer of meaning. It would be arbitrary to suppose that any one of these meanings which we choose to select is implied in any given context. The Greek *hustera* means 'womb', and although hysteria is not today understood as a disorder of that organ, this would not justify commentators on the fifth century B.C. taking its usage there as reflecting modern medical theories. Leucippus said that the world is composed of atoms, which is quite true if correctly interpreted, but untrue in the sense meant by Leucippus.

Polkinghorne of course affirms that the 'symbols' in the Bible have some reference to actual historical events. He believes that the story of the incarnation and the resurrection is not mere fiction, nor mere myth (myths being "a particular kind of symbol", p. 32), but has the "power" of both fact and myth (pp. 33, 63). But if this story, as detailed in the gospels, did really represent historical fact, it would not need this additional authentication. I suspect that he cannot quite bring himself to claim that the story is history pure and simple, and so takes his stand on an unclear position that falls short of this.

Such a half-way-house stance is not uncommon. In 1955, John Macquarrie maintained, on the one hand, that it is of no account whether historical investigations show the New Testament to be substantially reliable or not; for neither the theologian nor the ordinary believer should be "at the mercy of the historian". They are interested in "the mighty acts" in the gospels "in their character as saving events", which they cease to be when regarded as "objective-historical happenings". On the other hand, he has to allow that "there could only be saving events if there had been certain objective events"; and so he is at the mercy of the historian after all.[10]

All the apologists I have been discussing allow and even advocate multiple interpretations of the texts. The Bible, says Polkinghorne, "must be acknowledged as being polysemous, having multi-layered meanings capable of mediating many messages to its readers" (p. 67). He refers in this connection to "John Barton's notion of the 'semantic indeterminacy of sacred texts', which delivers us from too narrow a construal of their meaning and significance" (p. 2). Barton is in fact far from positive about this semantic indeterminacy and is aware that it can all too easily make texts what he calls "semantically vacuous". He gives, as an example, the way the Old Testament functioned in the early Church as "a *tabula rasa* on which Christians wrote what they took (on quite other grounds) to be the meaning of Christ". Their "hermeneutic" was "a set of devices that would extract edifying meanings from an unedifying text"; and "the modern interest in hermeneutics in theology is not so very different".[11] Quite so. One hears today talk of 'creative accounting', meaning 'fiddling the books'. It seems to be in the same sense that Barton speaks of "creative transcriptions", namely making "old words a peg on which to hang new ideas" (p. 77).

Polkinghorne calls the Bible "the supreme Christian classic" in the sense that any literary classic—he mentions Shakespeare and the Greek tragedians—"has something fresh to say to each new inquirer". When we read the Bible as history, we are concerned to find out whether it reports reliably, but when we read it as a classic, we are "submitting ourselves to it. . . . Our concern is not then analytical . . . but with the totality of what is set before us" (p. 66). This idea that the problems and perplexities of a text somehow vanish if one takes it as a whole is a common ploy. He quotes David Tracy in this connection: "Explicitly religious classic expressions will involve a claim to truth by the power of the whole—as in some sense a radical and finally gracious mystery".[12] 'Somehow'; 'in some (unspecified) way' or 'sense'—how often one meets these phrases in the apologists!

One reason why literary critics have come to hold that classics may ever be interpreted anew is that, so long as a conventional niche in the academic world continues to give economic encouragement to lecturers on literary classics, there must be something more for them to do than merely to repeat the insights of their predecessors. Polkinghorne allows that what some commentators have claimed to find both in the gospels and in Shakespeare has been "unduly imaginative".[13] He can, then, see that the freedom of individual interpretation which he advocates has its dangers. He has no sympathy with "allegorical extravagances", and says there must be no "wilful imposition" of meaning, but "sympathetic exploration". "The overplus of meaning is surely to be sought without undue strain"; and "the guidance of the Spirit" and beholdenness to the long tradition of mainstream Church exegesis will guard against aberration (p. 68). Unfortunately exegesis of which he approves includes features of that mainstream tradition which Barton has so justly criticized. For instance, as an example of appropriate "verbal fruitfulness blossoming within Scripture itself" (a New Testament writer giving a legitimate interpretation of an Old Testament passage), Polkinghorne mentions what the epistle to the Hebrews makes of words spoken, so he concedes, at the coronation of a king of Judah, namely "thou art a priest for ever, after the order of Melchizedek" (Psalm 110:4). In the understanding of the author of the epistle, these words were addressed to Christ (Hebrews 5:5–6). Polkinghorne does not go quite this far, but says that they trigger in the epistle a "sustained meditation on the eternal and effective priesthood of Christ" (p. 67). This is really to allow that a passage can mean what it suggests to someone who comes to it with his own predilections. He expressly affirms that the Bible "is not just there for our detached perusal, but as the vehicle for a personal encounter demanding a response" (p. 64). It invites us "to commit ourselves to sharing in that experience of the first Christians that 'if anyone is in Christ he is a new creation' (2 Corinthians 5:18)". It does indeed, but why should we respond positively to this invitation?

Polkinghorne's professional eminence has made him welcome to Christians. Paul Avis has noted that many of them, "without reading a word of his writings, . . . will be encouraged to know that a distinguished professional scientist is so firmly persuaded of the truth of the Christian faith". If they go on to peruse him, they may, with Avis, be a little disconcerted to find him advocating "a full-blooded, all or nothing, Christian theism, complete with the possibility of miracles and prayers for rain".[14] But in fairness one must allow, first that he realizes that theological beliefs are as provisional as scientific hypotheses: he emphasizes that "neither science nor theology can be pursued without a measure of intellectual daring, for neither is based on incontrovertible grounds of knowledge" (p. 1). Second, we shall see how frankly he admits himself baffled by the problem of undeserved suffering—a problem for any theist who believes in an omnipotent and all-loving deity.

II. Realists and Instrumentalists

Janet Soskice defines "theological realists" as those who, "while aware of the inability of any theological formulation to catch the divine realities", none the less accept that there are such realities; whereas "theological instrumentalists believe that religious language provides a useful, even uniquely useful system of symbols which is action-guiding for the believer, but not to be taken as making reference to a cosmos-transcending being in the traditional sense."[15]

The 'instrumentalist' position has sometimes been adopted because the reality of undeserved suffering was felt to rule out any acceptable 'realist' beliefs. John Polkinghorne, who is very much a 'realist' in Soskice's sense, confesses himself unable to make sense of undeserved suffering from his realist premisses. Many others have admitted to being similarly baffled (see, for instance, Ward's admission, p. 50 above), but Polkinghorne's statement of the issue is unusually frank and forceful, and particularly significant because of his professional eminence. He says:

> When we have subtracted all the great load of suffering which arises from man's inhumanity to man, there remains much which does not seem remotely to be our responsibility. To

whose charge is to be laid the severely handicapped child who will never have a normal human life? The thirty-year-old dying of cancer with half a life unfulfilled? The elderly person whose life ends in the prolonged indignity of senile dementia? If there is a God, surely these things must be his responsibility. It seems that either he who was thought of as the ground of the moral law is not himself wholly good, or he is opposed by other equal and conflicting powers in the world. Either way, the Christian understanding of God would lie in ruins.

I believe that this problem of theodicy, of understanding God's ways in the light of the mixture of goodness and terror which we find in the world, constitutes the greatest difficulty that people have in accepting a theistic view of reality. For those of us who stand within the Christian tradition, it remains a deep and disturbing mystery, nagging within us, of which we can never be unaware.[16]

The traditional Christian response to such suffering was that God's care of the world is beyond man's limited comprehension, and that what is apparently cruel is simply to be accepted as an element of this care. But, as Thomas Ogletree points out, this means that the believer in a loving God does not actually have different expectations concerning the facts and realities of life than one who denies the existence of a supreme being: "The only possible difference is that the believer may have a different attitude towards the facts"; and so, he says, some theologians have inferred from this that the word 'God', properly understood, refers not to any objective reality at all, but rather to "certain attitudes, feelings and expectations".[17]

It used to be widely believed that undeserved suffering in this life would at least be compensated in the next world, and there are passages in the New Testament which support such a view. But as Ward observes, decline in belief in life after death has, for many, closed this solution to the problem, and he thinks that this is why some theologians now "interpret theistic belief in terms of purely moral or attitudinal commitment".[18]

Foremost among the 'instrumentalists' of today is Don Cupitt. In his provocatively entitled *Taking Leave of God* (London: S.C.M., 1980), he holds that "God must be internalized", internalization being "the mighty historical process by which, over a period of many centuries, meanings and values were withdrawn from external reality and as it were sucked into the individual subject" (pp. 8, 39). God is "the mythical embodiment of all that one is concerned with in the spiritual life" (p. 120), a "unifying symbol that eloquently personifies and represents to us everything that spirituality requires of us"; and "the highest and central principle of spirituality"—he calls this principle "the religious requirement"—"is that we escape from 'craving' or 'carnal lusts'" and "become spirit", that is to say "attain the highest degree of self-knowledge and self-transcendence" (p. 9); and to achieve this we require myths:

> God is needed—but as a myth. We need myths because we are persons. A person is a process of becoming, and narrative is the literary form that best shows what persons are and can become. Persons all have life-stories, and indeed you might say that a person is just a story. Now the religious life is an inner

drama, the story of our response to the eternal religious requirement. It must be expressed in story-form, and religious stories are myths. Myth is the best, clearest and most effective way of communicating religious truth. (p. 120)

"It must be expressed in story-form" is a good example of the kind of dogmatism of which Cupitt's critics have complained; and the argument is quite incoherent: persons become, stories show persons becoming, the religious life is a becoming (a progress towards the spiritual) and therefore must have stories, and these need be no more than stories. Intelligent persons can write in this way only because, as words have almost entirely replaced ideas in their minds, they believe that verbal associations constitute reasoning and argument.

III. 'Narrative Theology'

Scholarly attempts to reconstruct the actual historical events (if any) underlying biblical accounts have yielded little that appeals to present-day believers. Much in the Old Testament has been shown to be myth. James Barr, writing on *The Bible in the Modern World* (London: S.C.M., 1973; reissued 1990) says that no serious participant in the discussion supposes that there were real events behind such stories as the flood that covered the world and wiped out all living things. There was, he adds, "no ark" and "no Jonah who fell into the sea and was swallowed by a fish" (p. 82). Similarly, the walls of Jericho did not collapse when the Israelites marched round the town seven times, with their priests blowing their trumpets (Joshua, Chapter 6). The excavations of Kathleen Kenyon showed that Jericho had lain in ruins long before any Israelites could have arrived there;[19] and Old Testament scholars have come to suppose that later generations, knowing that the place was a ruin, explained how this came about by a legend to the effect that God will always help his chosen people, by miraculous means if necessary. The story that Joshua burnt the city of Ai to the ground and exterminated its whole population, leaving it "the desolate ruined mount it remains to this day" (Joshua 8:28, NEB) obviously arose in the same way. Von Rad observes: "Excavations have demonstrated with certainty that Ai was abandoned already in the early Bronze Age and was first resettled only in the early Israelite era".[20]

If we turn from the Pentateuch to the Prophets, there are of course historical references in Isaiah and other prophetic literature, but these have been shown to be to ancient political and military squabbles, not to anything theologically edifying, such as the future coming of Jesus. As to what Jesus himself did and taught, there are as many opinions as there are scholars writing on the subject.[21]

Theologians have naturally been anxious to show that none of this really matters, and G.A. Lindbeck declares that the Bible "can be taken seriously as a delineator of divine and human agents, even when its history or science is challenged".[22] Hence the rise of what is known as 'narrative theology' which emphasizes that what matters for faith is the story the Bible tells, not any history that might lie behind it. H.W. Frei wants the "realistic or history-like quality" of many biblical narratives to be examined for "the bearing it has in its own right on meaning and interpretation", instead of being "transposed into the quite different issue of whether or not the realistic narrative [is] historical." He even holds that, because the writer of fiction, unlike the historian or biographer, has "direct or inside knowledge of his subjects", we are "actually in a fortunate position that so much of what we know about Jesus . . . is more nearly fictional than historical in narration".[23] Northrop Frye argues, in somewhat similar vein, that

> The events the Bible describes are what some scholars call 'language events', brought to us only through words; and it is the words themselves that have the authority, not the events they describe. The Bible means literally just what it says, but it can mean it only without primary reference to a correspondence of what it says to something outside what it says.[24]

In this kind of argument, as in some of those mentioned earlier in this chapter, the Bible is often said to resemble literary classics. Lindbeck says, of *Oedipus Rex* and *War and Peace,* that "they evoke their own domains of meaning . . . by what they themselves say about the events and personages of which they tell. To understand them in their own terms, there is no need for extraneous references to, for example, Freud's theories or historical treatments of the Napoleonic Wars" (p. 116). His standpoint really implies that there is really no need for "extraneous references" of any kind, that, as Frye has put it, it is the words themselves that have the authority.

In fact, however, we cannot understand Sophocles's play if we have no experiences, independent of it, that enable us to know what is meant by plague, murder, incest, infant exposure, and other incidents to which it refers. Words and sentences owe their power of conveying ideas solely to convention, which determines what real happenings or ideas the words stand for; and convention can establish itself readily only in the case of ideas or situations which are familiar. G.F. Stout, in the fifth edition of his *A Manual of Psychology* (London: University Tutorial Press, 1938 or later reprint), rightly insists that communication is based on shared experience (p. 537). He discusses the phrase 'Nansen skates' (p. 540), and, in spite of much technical terminology, really tells us no more than that two relatively vague words can lose some of their vagueness by being brought together. How this happens he leaves us to guess—perhaps because it is obvious that our knowledge of Nansen and of skates enables us to construct some kind of composite picture in which the two are united. If someone says 'gooseberry pie', I understand him because I am familiar with gooseberries and pies, and can envisage a particular complex involving them both. But if he were to say 'gooseberry skate', I should be unable to construct any complex from these components, simply because my experience fails me. For the common human affairs there is in general a set of agreed formulas, and in such cases it may be said that the words have a definite meaning which is not dependent on speaker or context. But when sentences have to be improvized for relatively novel purposes, for the expression, for instance of ideas not of familiar occurrence, then one must resort to new combinations. In such cases one falls back on experiment, and it may be necessary to try a number of alternatives before one finds a form of words which produce the effect aimed at. Such sentences as 'there is a mouse in the kitchen', or 'someone is at the front door' have a fairly precise and constant meaning in any domestic environment, and there will not as a rule be any need to vary the formula or explain the terms. But the situation is very different when we meet the metaphysical discourses of the fourth gospel, or the arguments in the epistle to the Romans. The indeterminate character of the words makes the task of the critic very difficult, for he has to decide whether his difficulties with them are due to his own imperfect education or to the author's imperfect logic. It is not meaningful to speak, as does a survey of recent biblical scholarship, of "the meaning of . . . texts as such", of "a relatively autonomous world of texts which have a communicative intention of their own", irrespective of human agents (author and readers).[25] For Lindbeck, however, what he calls his "cultural-linguistic approach" to theology means rejecting any "extratextual method which would locate religious meaning outside the text or semiotic system . . . in the objective realities to which it refers." For cultural linguists, he says, "the meaning is immanent" (p. 114).

The prevalence of ideas about language discussed earlier in this book has done much to favour such views. Lindbeck premises that the way a community interprets its environment depends on its cultural tradition, in particular on its language, the importance of which he exaggerates, confessing here to dependence on Chomsky and others from whom he accepts that "language . . . shapes domains of human existence and action that are pre-experiential" (p. 37). I know we cannot think without some kind of representations, vicarious or symbolic, but we can do so without verbal images, and can certainly free ourselves from the conventional restraints of any particular language. However, according to Lindbeck, for its adherents a given religion constitutes "a kind of cultural and/or linguistic framework that shapes the entirety of life and thought" and "functions somewhat like a Kantian *a priori*" (p. 33).[26] For the Christian, this framework is canonical scripture, and it determines how he understands not only the events of biblical times, but also those of his own: "To become a Christian involves learning the story of Israel and of Jesus well enough to interpret and experience one's world in its terms" (p. 34). It is the story as given in scripture that constitutes the lens through which the Christian perceives reality— not a critical interpretation of the story that disentangles from it actual events in Israelite or early Christian history. Scripture is not to be "translate[d] into extra-scriptural categories. It is the text, so to speak, which absorbs the world, rather than the world the text" (p. 118).

Non-Christian communities will naturally see things through the medium of other texts or speech. Hence, generalizing, Lindbeck declares: "To become religious involves becoming skilled in the language, the symbol system of a given religion" (p. 34). He admits that this may well seem "wholly relativistic", making different religions into "self-enclosed and incommensurable intellectual ghettos", and making the choice between them "purely arbitrary, a matter of blind faith" (p. 128). He tries to escape from such relativism by arguing that "the ultimate test" of the actual truth of a religion lies in "perfor-mance", that is, in the behaviour of those who believe it (p. 134). That 'Jesus is Lord' can be shown to be a true proposition only if those who speak the words are concerned to "do something about it", to commit themselves to "a way of life". This is what he means when he says, in a formulation characteristic of his far from lucid style, that "it is only through the performatory use of religious utterances that they acquire proposi-tional force" (p. 66). How this annuls relativism is unclear. Fanatics of very different persuasions commit themselves to ways of life. The terrorist, religiously or politically motivated, is capable of considerable self-sacrifice.

Lindbeck compares theological doctrines with grammatical rules (pp. 47, 84). "The abiding and doctrinally significant aspect of religion" consists in "the story it tells and in the grammar that informs the way the story is told and used" (p. 80). Thus a doctrine about God is a rule for appropriate use of the word, rather than a propo-sition about some entity. "The proper way to determine what 'God' signifies . . . is by examin-ing how the word operates within a religion", just as—so Lindbeck supposes—"hammers and saws . . . are made comprehensible by indicating how they fit into systems of communication or pur-poseful activity, not by reference to outside fac-tors" (p. 114). The phrase 'or purposeful activity' betrays that what is really involved is far more than mastering accepted linguistic usage. Some-one who has no idea of the functions of a hammer or a saw can be better helped by practical demon-stration of their use on materials than by learning how to use the words in accordance with estab-lished idiom. But for Lindbeck, to be a Christian is to master a "vocabulary" of "rites, stories, injunctions"—these form "a lexical core . . . found for the most part in the canonical scriptures"—and a "grammar" of church doctrines, "syntactical rules" which guide the use of the vocabulary in "constructing the world, community and self" (pp. 80–81). Although he claims that, like any grammatical rules, these may change over a period of time (p. 84), they include, for him, the traditional trinitarian and christological dogmas which, as Maurice Wiles has pointed out in criticism of him, are "immensely influential in determining how the biblical story is read", so that "even the possibility of any significant change in reading is ruled out in principle". Wiles adds: "The outcome is a retreat into the ghetto of a world created rather than illuminated by the scriptural text—indeed created by a particular way of reading the text".[27]

Similarly to Lindbeck, the Old Testament scholar B.S. Childs wants to avoid basing interpretations of scripture on what is extrinsic to the texts. He places his own interpretive work "within the context of modern discussion of the nature of language", and in this connection he uses Wittgenstein's phrase "language game".[28] This idea is obscure enough in Wittgenstein's own writings, and has, in the hands of some of his religious admirers, become what Anthony Kenny calls "a stone-wall defence against any demand for a justification of belief in God".[29] However, Childs's position remains finally unclear. Although he approves of Lindbeck's term " 'intratextuality' of meaning" as providing "a much needed service in checking the abuses of a crude theory of historical referentiality which has dominated biblical studies since the Enlightenment", he is nonetheless aware that "the concept is not without serious problems when used as a positive formulation of the Bible's relation to the external world". Christians, he adds, "have always understood that we are saved not by the biblical text, but by the life, death and resurrection of Jesus Christ who entered into the world of time and space".[30]

I have argued in previous chapters that it is quite absurd to try to understand reality by investigating language. Whether from one set of happenings we can infer or expect another is to be learned only from experience. A proposition is a reproduction of an experience, or of a type of experiences, its form depending on the language, but its substance on the experiences from which it is derived. If from one proposition another can be inferred, it is because experience has taught that the real events represented by the one are associated with those represented by the other. Two propositions are said to be contradictory when together they imply a combination of events or conditions which we know from experience do not occur in combination. However, the religious utility of restricting one's attention to language is obvious enough. If we do not need to ask whether what scripture alleges to have occurred really occurred at all, then we can bypass some very awkward questions. That this constitutes unacceptable evasion is conceded even by some of the sympathetic commentators on 'narrative theology'.[31]

I conclude this section by drawing attention to the views of a Glasgow theologian, Robert P. Carroll whose book *Wolf in the Sheepfold. The Bible as a Problem for Christianity* (London:

S.P.C.K., 1991) mentions something akin to the proposals of narrative theology as a "reading strategy" with which to deal with what is unacceptable, if taken at face value, in the Bible. Unlike so many of the others we have been studying, Carroll is not an apologist. He does not, finally, endorse anything like narrative theology; his book reflects his "deep puzzlement at the role the Bible plays in theology" (p. xi), and he is very well aware that it raises "profound problems" for the modern reader (p. 2).

One of his examples is the fierce antisemitism of so much of the New Testament. In Acts, orthodox Jews are represented as continually harassing and persecuting Christians. In the fourth gospel, Chapter 8, Jesus is made to say that the Jews have the Devil as father. In Matthew, Chapter 23, he mounts a savage attack on scribes and Pharisees, and in the passion narrative of this gospel the Jewish crowd cries out for Jesus's blood to be "on us and on our children" (27:24–25). In all four gospels Pilate appears as a kindly governor whose efforts to save Jesus's life are thwarted by Jewish malice. As a critical theologian, Carroll is well aware that all this is propaganda, not history, and that it reflects the interests of Christian communities of the late first century (when the gospels were written) in rivalry with Jewish ones occupying "the same social space" (p. 113), and competing for "power and position" (pp. 98–99). But he thinks that the modern reader may find all this antisemitism inoffensive if the Jews of the New Testament are understood as "belonging to the symbolic forms of that book". 'Jews' then becomes "a mythic term to describe rivalry and opposition": He continues:

This mode of constructing narratives gives them such a textuality ('intertextuality' would be a better description) that it would be very unwise to assume the texts have any referentiality *outside* themselves and the world of the text created by the older scriptures and the writers of the Gospels. Hence 'the Jews' of the New Testament are a nasty bunch of vicious people who killed Jesus and persecuted the Christians. Like wicked stepmothers in fairy tales or ogres in folk tales, such Jews are the stock in trade of Gospel story writing, but not to be confused with real, living people. (pp. 100–01)

Making the New Testament Jews in this way into mere "textual Jews" (p. 114) has the advantage of "resolving the insoluble problems of trying to relate the text to history". Moreover, as any competent reader of the passion narratives can see that they are "constructed from the Hebrew Bible, especially the lament Psalms", what connection need these narratives have with "any historical circumstances"? Paul, whose record is the earliest extant, merely says that Christ died, was buried, and was raised (1 Corinthians 15:1–4); and this left the evangelists "ample room" for developing an imaginative account—"a sustained narrative of plot and counterplot, conspiracy and denial, power plays and cowardice" (pp. 101–02).

Carroll apparently accepts—I presume on the authority of Paul and other Christian writers earlier than the gospels—that Jesus was crucified (p. 102. He is certainly not relying on Jewish corroboration of this testimony, as he allows that "we have nothing in Jewish sources" about Jesus "which could reliably be dated to the first century", p. 100). But Paul and these other pre-gospel

Christian writers do not know of the crucifixion as a recent event in a known setting. They know nothing of the time, place, or circumstances of Jesus's sojourn on earth and subsequent return to heaven, and what they say on the matter has no more the aspect of historical reportage than what had been alleged of other figures during the inter-testamental period. Carroll himself cannot accept the third of Paul's three items in 1 Corinthians 15 (for Paul the really important one), namely the resurrection—at any rate not in any sense intended by Paul. For Carroll calls the resurrection "a profoundly puzzling tale" which he can "only deal with in terms of symbolic forms" (p. 135).

The "reading strategy" which Carroll is discussing involves taking much in the New Testament as mere rhetoric, modelled on the way people are vilified in the prophetic books of the Hebrew Bible. There:

> people are never accused of making mistakes or failing to live up to an ideal, they are accused of adultery and murder, of worshipping false gods and lying, of cannibalism and robbery. . . . This type of rhetorical overkill is such a feature of biblical writing that it is difficult not to read Matthew 23 as one more instance of it. . . . The rant factor being so dominant in prophecy, it would be a pity to render the rhetoric prosaic by matching it to a social reality. . . . Hence the scribes and Pharisees of Matthew 23 are not to be confused with real flesh and blood Jews but are to be seen as characters in a world constructed by the text (pp. 104–05).

But in the end Carroll seems to acknowledge that this really will not do. We know from modern novels how fact and fiction can be combined by using real historical characters as figures in fiction writing, but "whether we should apply such an analysis to ancient writings may be a more difficult question to answer". "Modern readings of ancient texts cannot escape history quite as easily" (pp. 101–02). And so theologians have yet to find a way of making the Bible acceptable. In the next (final) section of this chapter, we shall study the frank admissions of some of them on this matter.

IV. The Bible Without Binding Authority

It is generally recognized that the situation which has arisen since the onset of biblical criticism at about the end of the eighteenth century demands of Christians what Dennis Nineham has called "a different relationship to the Bible from any appropriate or possible before". He adds: "Most theologians would also agree that no fully appropriate relationship has yet been discovered or defined."[32] Leslie Houlden voices the same frank and honest uncertainty when he declares that "modern New Testament study . . . has made the New Testament no longer usable in ways long established in Christian devotion", so that it is "not . . . determinative for present belief".[33] The sayings and deeds of personages in both Old and New Testaments have come to be seen as the outcome of a sometimes long process of editing and transmission, so that the distinction the Protestants of the Reformation period insisted on, between scripture as binding and tradition as not, can no longer be sustained: scripture is itself the outcome of variegated tradition.

Biblical scholarship has shown that the New Testament yields no uniform teaching. Paul's views are reworked by later epistle writers within the canon, writing under his name. Pauline teaching (or what the writer takes for such) is controverted in the letter of James, is declared in the second epistle of Peter to be "hard to understand" and in fact to have been grossly misunderstood. The Acts of the Apostles presents Paul in a very different light from that in which he appears in his own writings. The thought of Mark is adapted by Matthew, and in a different way by Luke. The thought of the Johannine church, as represented in the fourth gospel, is significantly different from what it is in the epistles ascribed to John; and the fourth gospel diverges very substantially from all three of the others. There are considerable differences concerning the nature as well as the doctrines of Jesus. What the Christian's relation to the Jew should be—rejection or qualified acceptance—is a matter to which different canonical passages give different answers. Whether one should renounce family ties or cultivate them also depends on which passages one consults, as does what one's attitude to possession of wealth should be, and how far one should extend love to those of other persuasions. Houlden sums this up with: "New Testament ethics varies from writer to writer", quite apart from the fact that Christian tradition gives little or no guidance on many important present questions (pp. 165–66).[34]

In many cases, canonical writers were themselves well aware that they were opposing the doctrines of other Christians—even, as already indicated, doctrines that are now included in the canon. John Fenton has shown that "twenty-four out of the twenty-seven New Testament books are to varying degrees the result of controversy among Christians", that is to say, "eighty-nine percent of the New Testament is the result of Christian disagreement", which was sometimes "extremely bitter". The three books without such controversy are concerned either with controverting the Jews (1 Thessalonians), or with conflict with pagan persecutors (1 Peter), or with a matter between author and recipient (Philemon).[35]

Maurice Wiles thinks that, in view of all this, Christians should no longer regard scripture as "a binding authority", and should come to see it rather as "an indispensable resource". For him, the diversity and conflict that has been with Christianity from its inception is not something wholly ill; for "if the truth by which we are to live is not authoritatively given in the past, but continually to be discovered in the present, such a process of discovery is bound to involve experimentation, with attendant error and conflict."

Wiles realizes that, if his approach to scripture is accepted, the church will not be able to give definitive rulings on the virgin birth or the bodily resurrection of Christ, among other doctrines, in the way it has done in the past. His critics, he says, may object that he is placing scripture under the tyranny of the scholar (who has done so much to raise awkward questions about its value). To this he replies, appositely, that "what the scholar does is only a more concentrated form of what is involved in any reflective reading of scripture— and it cannot be the church's goal to exclude that".[36]

The way in which the scholar simply carries further the careful reading of the layman is well illustrated by James Barr, apropos of the well-known theory that the opening books of the Old Testament are a fusion of four principal documents (called J, E, D, and P), some of which are hundreds of years older than others. He mentions the familiar instance that one passage in Genesis makes Ishmael a small child when Hagar was driven into the wilderness: Abraham "put him on her shoulder" and later, when she was exhausted, she 'threw' or 'thrust' him under a bush (21:14–15). Genesis 17:25, however, makes Ishmael already 13 years old even before Isaac was born. Barr comments that a critical separation of sources is a very natural way of explaining the discrepancy:

> The genealogical material of Ch. 17 (P) was written independently of the personal story about Hagar and does not fit with it. Observation of hundreds of such discrepancies patiently pieced together over a long period, and valued as evidence precisely because the scholars did not allow defensive and harmonizing interpretations to push aside the literal sense of the text, led to the critical reconstruction.[37]

Like Wiles, Houlden argues for a certain "provisionality" in religious beliefs, although he is aware that such tentativeness is not what we find in the Bible, where both the classical prophets of Israel and Jesus speak and act with urgency and authority. Houlden does not want tentativeness to be impaired by "sticking-points"—by, for instance, insistence on traditional doctrines such as the resurrection or the trinity (pp. 35–36). Yet he is aware that Christianity must have some christological doctrine if it is not to become mere theism. "To be a Christian is to accord to Jesus unique significance in our relationship with God" (p. 132). How this is to be done, he does not pretend to say.

I have the highest regard for all the writers I have mentioned in this section of this chapter. But I think that, in trying to retain justifiable religious significance for the figure of Jesus, they have undertaken a hopeless task.

The biblical criticism that has led to all this questioning of the Bible's authority has greatly increased our understanding of Judaism and early Christianity. But is there any loss that goes with this gain? Discarding traditional beliefs has had disruptive effects in the past. Gilbert Murray said that anthropology seems to show that "inherited conglomerates" (his term for tradition, tribal custom, taboos, and superstitions) "have practically no chance of being true or even sensible; and, on the other hand, that no society can exist without them or even submit to any drastic correction of them without social danger."[38] Approval by one's fellows and fear of censure are among society's chief integrating forces; but if they are to be effective as such forces, there must exist a climate of opinion, a common attitude of approval and disapproval towards certain forms of behaviour. If this attitude is not universal, or nearly so, its influence on the individual is much diminished. In a community where it is permissible to put everything into question, the climate of opinion becomes unsettled, and certain acts are no longer universally approved or disapproved, so that the ordinary person's main motive for social behaviour is very much weakened.

Today, not only biblical but all kinds of authority have come to be questioned—not (at any rate not principally) as a result of the impact of biblical criticism, but as a reaction against crass instances of abuse of authority by those exercising it. Barr notes that the questioning affects legal systems, governments, teachers, and professors, and "last but not least . . . parents and the older generation, as members of it are painfully aware."[39] While we do not wish for subservience to undeserving authorities, we cannot rest content with anything like anarchy. There is a problem here for the atheist as well as for the Christian. Man is a social animal; he cannot now exist except in some form of community, and so his behaviour must be adapted to social conditions. Human instincts have been developed in accordance with this necessity, in that, while we certainly possess instincts which prompt us to defend our own interests against rivals, we also have instincts which prompt us to protect some at least of our associates. However, even if we ignore the special promptings of instinct in our theorizing on ethical matters, we can see that it is in our interest that there should be certain general rules of behaviour within our community to protect us from injury or exploitation. We must also see that, if these rules are to be generally adhered to, every individual must respect them, and therefore we ourselves must respect them. Nevertheless, it has to be admitted that there are circumstances in which it is appropriate to break them. 'Thou shalt not kill' is a good rule, but was it wrong of Hitler's generals to try, in 1944, to blow him to pieces? In sum: no rules at all would make life in society totally insecure; completely inflexible rules will lead to much unnecessary suffering; yet how can one allow exceptions without breaking down the consensus on which stability depends?

Naturally, attempts are made to show that the 'inherited conglomerate' of traditional Christian beliefs has not been as extensively damaged as its critics within the Church suppose. David L. Edwards tries to counter colleagues such as Nineham and Wiles in his *Tradition and Truth,* a discussion of radical English theology of the past 25 or so years, published by Hodder and Stoughton in 1989. He wonders whether "Christian believing will remain so often and so tragically polarised between [such] radical explorers and conservative worshippers" (p. 263). People, he rightly observes, "want religion to be a rock, not a crumbling sandcastle"; they "do not want to be walking question marks following in the steps of a crucified enigma" (p. 256). He generously allows his own attempts to restore some hardness to the rock to be followed, as the ending to his book, by severe responses from the radicals to his criticisms of them. Wiles there finds some of Edwards's arguments to be forms of words to which he can attach no meaning, and complains that he "ends up by simply repeating the orthodox rhetoric" (p. 290). Wiles instances the discussion (on p. 156) of the opening verses of Luke's gospel, where Edwards speaks of poetry which celebrates the birth of Jesus as something that "began in the heart of God, for 'the power of the Most High' overshadowed that life before Jesus spoke a word"; and he mentions Edwards's statements (pp. 160, 165) that "whatever Jesus . . . did . . . it is really God that did it in Jesus", and that there is "salvation in Jesus from God". Apropos of Edwards's allowing for some, admittedly limited, number of divine interventions in answer to prayer, he comments: "Do not many of the often claimed acts of God in response to prayer . . . seem trivial compared with those evils that appear to have been allowed to continue unchecked by divine action, frequently despite much believing prayer?" This is a point of some importance in the present-day situation, where the efficacy of prayer is frequently put forward as a decisive ground for belief in God—Daphne Hampson's recent book is a striking example.[40]

It is no arbitrary wantonness but years of study that have driven the 'radical explorers' among theologians old and new to positions of uncertainty. This is particularly clear from Nineham's response to Edwards. He compares (p. 297) his own experience to that of his tutor R.H. Lightfoot—"a traditionalist by temperament if ever there was one", who was nevertheless "forced by years of gospel study to the conclusion that 'the form of the earthly no less than that of the heavenly Christ is for the most part hidden from us'". Nineham adds that, for the authors of the New Testament,

> edification was a value in writing about the past at least as important as accuracy, which was in any case impossible for them, at any rate to anything like the degree to which we demand it today. As they saw it, to have written an account of the past which did not conform with the religious beliefs of their time would have seemed irresponsible, whatever the available evidence might be. Indeed lack of conformity with current religious belief would have seemed to them a sure sign of falsity in any report, however strong its external attestation might be. (p. 300)

The attitude Nineham here specifies is—with some *mutatis mutandis*—so common as to be almost ineradicable. We all have a framework onto which we fit experiences that come our way, and few of us are prepared seriously to question its composition.[41] 'Facts not in accordance with revolutionary theory are not true facts' say, or used to say, the modern political equivalents of the New Testament evangelists. R.W. Numbers's recent book *The Creationists: The Evolution of Scientific Creationism* (New York: Knopf, 1992) shows how many participants in the relevant debate "viewed the world through distinctive 'sets of spectacles' that uniquely colored everything in sight" (p. 207). People acquire a strong prejudice in favour of any view, however cheerful or however gloomy, which they themselves have originated or defended. It may have been adopted reluctantly, but once someone has associated it with himself, with his own reputation, he gets a special liking for it that has no connection with its intrinsic merits.

❧ 5
Mental Adaptation

The final section of the previous chapter has raised issues—about religious beliefs and about ethical ideas—that are not directly bound up with problems relating to language. In the present, final chapter I wish to continue this more general approach by attempting an account, not restricted to the rôle of language, of mankind's propensities to error. I shall, however, finally note how these can be exacerbated by language.

When we compare the behaviour of the antelope with that of the gorilla, we find a great many important differences, but taking a broad view, biologists can give some account of the evolution which led to this differentiation of characters from a theoretical common ancestor. Ungulates have specialized their locomotive at the expense of their manipulative apparatus, and this is understandable because they live in open country where speed of movement is often the best protection from powerful enemies and range of movement the best guarantee of an unfailing food supply. Climbing animals, on the other hand, protected from predators which cannot leave the ground, developed manipulative behaviour. We may suppose that the ungulate specialization of locomotion, leading to the establishment of rhythmical reflexes of the four limbs, involved only relatively simple nervous mechanisms, whereas the power of independent movement in the limbs, and even in the digits, encouraged by the practice of climbing, would require and stimulate an increase in brain complexity.

It may be that if either the antelope or the gorilla could reflect on the differences between them, he would judge them to be very great indeed; but we, from a fairly impartial standpoint, can see the common elements which underlie both characters. When, however, we compare the behaviour of any mammal with that of man, we are much more impressed by the differences than with the resemblances; and this tendency has been encouraged by philosophical and religious preconceptions.

In fact, the doctrine of man's unique place in the universe is hard to reconcile with a zoological conception of the human race. Barbour mentions both biological and fossil discoveries which indicate that human beings and modern African apes are descended from common ancestors: "African chimpanzees and gorillas share more than 99 percent of their DNA with that of human beings (which would be comparable to the genetic kinship of horses and zebras or dogs and foxes)." He adds that the move from trees to grassland seems to have encouraged both upright posture and a shift to hunting; for footprints four million years old of the apelike *Australopithecus afarensis* are consistent only with upright posture; and the teeth of 'Lucy', a short female who "walked on two legs but had long arms and a brain size like that of the great apes", show that she was a meat eater. In the opinion of many human palaeontologists upright posture, by freeing the hands for more delicate manipulative use (and thus facilitating acquaintance with the functions and properties of objects) encouraged expansion and further elaboration of the brain; and such development is evidenced in *Homo habilis* who, says Barbour, "was present two million years ago . . . and chipped stones to make primitive tools".[1]

Pace Hegel and other metaphysicians, thinking is not peculiar to man, though his thoughts are more elaborate and play a more important part in his behaviour.[2] Every mammal gets to know its environment well enough for its needs. Man's scientific knowledge is more extensive but not otherwise different from the gorilla's knowledge of his forest and its other inhabitants.

Broadly speaking there are two ways in which an animal can become adapted to its environment. Many birds and insects whose eyes do not permit them to carry on their normal activities in darkness become adapted to nocturnal conditions by roosting or creeping into shelter until daylight returns, thus avoiding the effects of the unfavourable condition. Other birds and some insects have developed eyes or other senses which make them independent of daylight, and they are as much at home, or more so, during the night as during the day. The former type of animal adapts his behaviour so as to avoid the unfavourable condition, the latter adapts his body so that the condition ceases to be unfavourable.

Ideas of evolution, which have done so much to give direction and method to biological investigations, fail almost entirely in the anthropological sciences, since we are here dealing with changes which involve non-heritable characters.[3] Human culture belongs to those forms of behaviour which are learned by the individual, and must therefore be explained by reference to the psychological principles which underlie habits and traditions. What has been discovered of extinct manlike animals suggests that the principal anatomical features of man—in particular the upright posture and the enlarged brain—were already developed before any process of cultural development began. Barbour adds to the details already mentioned that *Homo habilis* was followed by *Homo erectus* of 1.6 million years ago, who "lived in long-term group sites, made more complicated tools and probably used fire". He continues:

> Archaic forms of *Homo sapiens* appeared 500,000 years ago, and the Neanderthals were in Europe 100,000 years ago. The Cromagnans made paintings on cave walls and performed burial rituals 30,000 years ago. Agriculture goes back only 10,000 years. The earliest known writing, Sumerian, is 6,000 years old. Techniques for melting metallic ores brought the Bronze Age and then, less than 3,000 years ago, the Iron Age.

If man cannot readily adapt his body, he can avoid unfavourable conditions by changing them. He cannot grow warm fur or long teeth and claws, but he can make clothes and sharp weapons. He cannot avoid the cold by winter sleep, but he can build shelter and make a fire. The great development of his brain makes possible a further kind of adaptation. As we saw, mammals in general have acquired to a marked extent the power of recognizing situations, objects, and events from many different points of view; but man has carried this capacity to the point where he is able, from a brief glimpse of some object, to relate it to a whole system of knowledge and, with the aid of this, in a short time to reconstruct the past and predict some of the future of the object of which he has had such a fleeting view. As a result, he has come to look before and after to a much greater extent than any other mammal.

One consequence of looking into the less immediate future and guiding behaviour by distant expectations is a willingness to endure discomfort and labour for the sake of some anticipated good. Any animal, if he is to learn to behave in a particular way, must be rewarded whenever he does so until the habit is acquired. But unlike dogs, human beings will often be satisfied with a promise, and it is only necessary that they should feel confident that it will be honoured. The dog must get his biscuit regularly if he is to learn the trick that brings his master to supply it, whereas a man has only to be persuaded that it is coming. In such a case his adaptation is mental, and so we may say that with man, as with other animals, there are two kinds of adaptation, though not the same kinds as with them: the one kind involves altering his environment to suit his needs, the other convincing himself that in the long run all will be well. In my own case, I find I can get thoroughly warmed to my work only when I have the feeling (or the illusion) that I am advancing toward some goal. As soon as the notion arises that the effort is vain, my energy flags and my interest fades away; but if only the feeling of success—even if it is an illusion— can be maintained, then more energy becomes available.

In fact man lives in a world created to some

extent by his own brain, and his happiness depends on the kind of world he creates there. The world as he believes it to be is more important for him than the world as it is, provided only that his belief is not in danger of being shaken by events; and that will depend on a number of factors, among which how often and how severely the belief is tested by experience is an important, but not necessarily decisive one. Sociologists have shown that "when people are committed to a belief and a course of action, clear disconfirming evidence may simply result in deepened conviction and increased proselytizing"— particularly if the believer is not an isolated individual, but a member of a group of persons who can support each other.[4] We do not even need recent sociological studies to establish this, as we have long been familiar with Christians who still believe that Jesus is coming soon and with communists who retained their faith in Soviet Russia. Admittedly, disconfirming evidence may eventually become so overwhelming that a belief collapses, but in many cases clear and decisive evidence is simply not forthcoming. Someone "could not long continue to believe that he could live on air or that it never rained on Thursdays, but he might go through life believing that the sun is not much bigger than the moon; and where beliefs concern the remote past or the remote future, there is, in the case of most men, little to prevent them believing almost anything".[5] Hence it comes about that man, the cleverest of all the animals, is also the most prone to fantastic errors.

Religions—Judaism, Christianity, and Islam are obvious examples—commonly guide behaviour by reference both to a remote past and to a remote future. In terms of the two forms of human adaptation, we may say that on the whole science aims at altering the environment, whereas religion—and much philosophy too—aim at altering belief. The scientist enables us to some extent to escape from adversity, the theologian and the philosopher teach us to endure it. (Liberation theology is an unusual exception.)

When something has been explained, we understand why it has happened and are better able to expect and prepare for its occurrence another time. We also know better what is likely to follow it, and how far its consequences are likely to injure or benefit us. However, the practical significance of any explanation may be very indirect. Historical explanations, for instance, do not generally affect our behaviour very much. Explanations of past events, and of present conditions in terms of past events, are often undertaken rather to bring them into harmony with our settled convictions than to base any important behaviour on them. An account which flatters or comforts us is in these cases preferred to one which does the reverse. The history of our own country or party or church is expounded in such a way as to support our partialities and sympathies, and such accounts often have no other purpose and no other use. Much of the doctrine in religion is of this kind, as is, perhaps surprisingly, admitted by some of its apologists. R.P.C. Hanson, for instance (sometime bishop and Professor of Divinity), having asked "why should we believe the word witnessed to by the Bible and taught by the Church to be true?", replied: "What more attractive and satisfying account can be found of our destiny, purpose and status in the world? . . . What makes believers believe is the attractiveness of the proposition which the Christian faith presents to us". He did not, of course, maintain that the only criterion for the truth of a theory is the pleasure to be derived from it: but he does say that "if we start from this point", we shall find other kinds of authority for the Christian faith "falling into place". We ask, for instance, if we know any "better account of things" than this "attractive and satisfying one", and whether any alternative "engage[s] our minds at the deepest level".[6] Pseudo-psychological notions such as 'levels' of the mind are common accessories in such writing, where an imposing vocabulary goes with questionable ideas. In an earlier book, Hanson had been justly critical of eminent Christian writers of the first two centuries because they "very readily attributed to apostolic tradition any custom or rite or tradition which they could not find directly referred to in the Bible and which they thought to be older than living memory".[7] But these early Christians were thereby only offering what was for them—in the wording of the principle advocated by Hanson himself—the most 'attractive and satisfying account' of things.

Other emotional factors are often of importance in such apologetics. A belief can be supported equally well by desire or fear. We believe quite readily not only what we wish to be true, but also what we fear may be true. Grounds for belief are insufficient to make someone suggestible: there must also be absence of alternatives, and this may result from poverty of ideas, from ignorance, from a narrow field of consciousness which prevents other ideas from entering the mind to compete with the first, even if they are available in the memory. In the case of beliefs held with passionate conviction, predisposition may be a significant factor, as it often is with the passions of love or anger. The young person is in a physiological state which may lead to an approach to another individual who, at a later time and on more mature reflection, would exercise no attraction. In the same way, anger may depend not only on the exciting stimulus, but also on a predisposition. A scornful remark may produce but a mild effect of resentment under many circumstances; if, however, it is but the latest of a number of offensive comments, especially if they are all from the same person, it may cause an explosion which to the onlooker seems quite out of proportion to the occasion. So with fear. When one is expecting to be attacked and aware of danger, a small and harmless incident may give rise to a panic action. Tinbergen illustrates how the reactions of birds and fish under the influence of powerful internal states are released by trivial stimuli which under more normal conditions would have little or no effect.[8]

Another significant emotional factor is the fascination of what is surprising or horrific. Delight in horror stories is to some extent based on an insatiable thirst for the thrill of horror, and old-style hellfire sermons could exploit this as well as the emotion of fear. As for surprise and wonder, these, as Hume long ago noted in his famous essay 'Of Miracles', are often agreeable emotions; and his contemporary James Lind, in his *A Treatise of the Scurvy,* made this factor partly responsible for the persistence of absurd ideas. It had been seriously argued that mice sprang from mud, and could be created by putting wheat or cheese with dirty rags. Lind commented on such 'spontaneous generation':

> There would indeed be some difficulty in conceiving how men of such wild fancies . . .

could ever get into possession of that degree of fame which they have acquired, did we not experience how much the world is disposed to admire whatever surprises: as if we were endued with faculties to see through ordinary follies, while great absurdities strike with an astonishment which overcomes the powers of reason, and makes improbability even an additional motive to belief.[9]

As we saw in the case of R.P.C. Hanson, some apologists do not find anything wrong with a strongly emotional basis to religious beliefs. This attitude has sometimes been prompted by awareness that attempts to study religion have so often led to the discrediting of it; and if this result is feared by people who are unwilling to give up their beliefs they naturally avoid examining them too closely. However, no one can any longer suppose that it is possible to impose the doctrines of any one religion on the rest of the world; and so any community's beliefs and ideals are best supported by an appeal to facts and to reason: if they are based on reality, they will be more useful to believers and are more likely to seem plausible to others. One reason why people love a mystery is that what is not known may be the subject of anybody's conjecture. Our conception of the world has to be fitted into the framework of known facts, and the more gaps there are in this framework, the more freedom we seem to have in conceiving the world, whereas every solution of a mystery robs us of some of this liberty.

I have earlier emphasized the strength of man's tendency to extend the scope of generalizations he has reached from observation of particular instances (cf. above, pp. 141 f). This is certainly a factor which greatly facilitates acceptance of comforting theories. We saw that such extension of a generalization is to some extent to be observed in other mammals;[10] indeed, it is an indispensable element in the process of learning. No situation ever recurs exactly, and so an animal, learning to correlate one situation with another on the basis of their being repeatedly conjoined, must not be too particular in identifying instances of the first, but must be content with a general similarity to it as previously experienced. On this basis, he may take situation X, now confronting him, as another instance of a familiar situation A, which previous experience has told him will lead to B. If he is wrong, if the similarity between what he is now experiencing (X) and what he has learnt to recognize as A is not close enough to warrant his generalization, then his error, if not fatal, is likely to be corrected by further experience: he learns that not any A but only an A where certain elements are present will lead to B. Animals other than man can have most of their errors corrected in this way because the situations which interest them are relatively simple and limited, and because they are interested only in the *immediate* results of their reactions to these situations. Man, however, has many beliefs where corrective experience is not forthcoming. The futile practices of magic illustrate his persisting belief in correlations between certain of his actions and certain remote results: the practices survive because the bond between action and result is remote enough to prevent the failure of the latter from inhibiting the former (cf. above, p. 140).

One of the arguments in Peter Berger's book *A Rumour of Angels* (Harmondsworth: Penguin, 1969) relies expressly on uncorrected generalizing. A child, he says, may wake up in the night, perhaps from a bad dream, and is then assured by its mother that "everything is all right". If this is not to be called a lie, there must, says Berger, be "some truth in the religious interpretation of human experience"; for the mother's reassurance, "transcending the immediately present two individuals and their situation, implies a statement about reality as such", namely that "*everything* is in order"—a formula which "can, without in any way violating it, be translated into a statement of cosmic scope", namely "have trust in being". This, he says, is "precisely what the formula intrinsically implies", and this in turn implies ultimate salvation in a blessed immortality; for "if there is no other world, then the ultimate truth about this one is that eventually it will kill the child as it will kill his mother." Hence "the parental role is not based on a loving lie. On the contrary, it is a witness to the ultimate truth of man's situation in reality". He summarizes this argument as follows:

> In the observable human propensity to order reality there is an intrinsic impulse to give cosmic scope to this order, an impulse that implies not only that human order in some way corresponds to an order that transcends it, but that this transcendent order is of such a character that man can trust himself and his destiny to it. (pp. 72–75)

Thus a religious doctrine is not only based on, but is proved true by man's 'impulse' to premature generalization! Berger, well-known as a sociologist, says he wrote this book in order to "comfort theologians" (p. 55). It is hard to believe that they will find much by way of comfort in this example of his reasoning (although Robert Runcie, Archbishop of Canterbury until his recent retirement, accepts it.[11]) It does, however, show how the 'impulse' in question can lead to the kind of arbitrariness that could hardly have been even contemplated, had it not been found so flattering to human aspirations.

There are, however, factors which militate against acceptance of comforting theories—in particular awareness of facts which run counter to them. John Macquarrie would fain believe that a "godless world" is "essentially absurd"; for our world is "ordered and structured", not "just chaos", and has also "brought forth spiritual and personal beings", all of which makes atheism "a most improbable thesis". There are, then, in his view, certain features in the world that would not be there if it had not been made by God. With the general acceptance of the Darwinian theory, this argument has lost much of its force; hence many believers prefer to claim that their knowledge of God derives from personal encounter with a personal being, rather than from deistic inferences about the nature of the world. Macquarrie himself, in spite of his confidence in the implications of an ordered world, cannot shut his eyes to "suffering, waste and apparent aimlessness", and allows that, in the face of these, "the world remains ambiguous" and "it is hard to believe in God."[12]

Another example of how difficult mental adaptation can be in the face of awkward facts is provided by the many writers who want to attribute much or all of the hatefulness and misery of the world to ungodliness, but are aware of how often evil has been worked by religious persons. J.H. Mahaffy, the well-known Irish classical scholar who died in 1919, wrote a *Survey of Greek Civilization* (London: Macmillan, 1897) in which he purports to contrast Greek "culture of intellect without moral forces to balance it" with the culture which has "received the powerful support of Christianity" (pp. vi–vii). Yet he goes on to admit that "the Italian states in the Renaissance of the fifteenth and sixteenth centuries were torn by all the vices and crimes which Thucydides describes as rife in the warring Greek republics", and that "even in the present day" atrocities are committed "such as we might only expect from the savages of Central Africa". He adds:

> Do we not see greed, ambition, international jealousy urging neighbour nations to cast aside every moral, every Christian consideration, and to draw the sword in support of national objects which every honest man in either nation would disavow as base and unworthy in any private transaction? So far one might be tempted to say that the teaching of Christianity has made, alas! but little difference.

The whole paragraph shows an eminent historian struggling to maintain a strong prejudice, in spite of blatant facts of human history.

The less sophisticated can achieve mental adaptation by simply ignoring evidence which would compromise it. As the theologian Leslie Houlden has said, "untenability is rarely a mortal disease in theology and often the patient never notices it."[13] This is certainly the situation in the popular preaching and evangelizing of the Churches, in marked contrast to the concessions and reservations of many of their theologians, generations of whom have accepted that teachings and behaviour ascribed to Jesus in the four canonical gospels represent a medley of material —some of it morally unacceptable—constructed by conflicting early Christian communities, each one of which was thereby trying to authenticate its own doctrines. But preachers and teachers of the young persist in representing any New Testament incident or teaching that happens to suit them as historically accurate, while anything from the same documents that they find less edifying is ignored or sometimes even misrepresented. While a learned theologian tries to come to terms with what he calls "the crude and embarrassing problem of the gospel miracles",[14] a recent report, anxious to justify the evangelizing of children, finds Jesus's proximity to them reliably documented, because "the boy with the loaves and fishes was obviously close at hand (John 6:9)". The same report is pleased to note the assurance of "an experienced children's evangelist" that children can "grasp the concept" that "doing what Jesus says makes for a better way of life".[15] There is no indication here that a better way of life can result from implementing only a very selective compilation of the precepts ascribed to Jesus in the gospels, and that such selectivity would have to be justified. Nor is there any awareness of the difficulties biblical scholars have encountered in achieving any such justification. Nineham speaks for many of them when he observes that "if . . . we are asked to pattern our life and beliefs on the teaching and attitude of Jesus, it is not at all clear that we have sufficient evidence to be sure what his attitude or teaching was".[16] A Jewish contributor to an interesting symposium entitled *Is Christianity Credible?* has quite correctly noted that "such creeds as the divine nature of Jesus, the virgin birth and the resurrection, as examples of the kind of beliefs which a Jew would find incredible, have already been called into question, if not rejected, by leading Christian theologians."[17] But one would never gather this from the report from which I have been quoting, which places the focus of evangelism on "the understanding that Jesus is God come among us", and accepts only resignedly that in our state schools "the Resurrection is not treated as an unchallenged historical event such as the Battle of Hastings" (pp. 15, 24).

Not that theologians critical of traditional orthodoxy agree among themselves. Although Alan Sell has recently complained of people who "feel entitled to 'know better' than the theologian in a way in which they would never dream of 'knowing better' than a nuclear physicist or neurologist",[18] there has in fact never, since Christianity's inception, been a doctrine of 'the theologian' which can be humbly accepted, only conflicting doctrines of rival theologians. I am not suggesting that this in any way discredits theology —only that it precludes the kind of deference that Sell wishes to see. Disagreement between persons studying the same things occurs at every turn in science and in everyday life. In a subject such as theology, where decisive evidence is in any case difficult to come by, there are bound to be sharp differences of opinion, and these will be even sharper where, as is so often the case, faith is reckoned to be as important as reason for determining the truth. Admittedly, there has been, among the more liberal proponents, a modicum of agreement indicated by progressive surrender of traditional positions. Houlden notes that the liberalism typified in Bishop Charles Gore in the

1890s "extended to taking the Genesis stories down to Abraham as unhistorical", and to treating Jesus's humanness more realistically than had usually been the case; but "it did not extend to thinking that Anglican clergy might preach in Nonconformist church halls or that Anglican bishops need not believe in the virgin birth or the physical resurrection of Jesus"—as, he adds, Hensley Henson (the Bishop of Durham who died in 1947) "discovered in relation to both matters". Since then, things have moved on considerably, and Houlden is able to record that, although the publication of *The Myth of God Incarnate* in 1977 occasioned an outcry asserting the classical doctrine of the incarnation, in the meantime the main contentions of that book have been quietly assimilated "by osmosis", in that "writers claiming attachment to the traditional faith have come to express themselves in terms essentially at one with the main thrust" of the authors of *The Myth*.[19]

However much one may welcome such relaxation of dogma evident in many (but by no means all) theologians of today, one unfortunate result of this progressive erosion of what has traditionally been believed has been a growing tendency to avoid any confrontation with countervailing facts by constructing attractive beliefs that are too vague to collide with reality. Perhaps this is, quite generally, the most common way of achieving mental adaptation. Colin Buchanon (until recently Bishop of Aston) tells us that, at the crucifixion, "in some mysterious and imagination-defying way, the sins of the world were taken into the body, indeed into the person of Jesus".[20] If some particular combination of ideas is not capable of being represented in the mind—as, for example, two groups of three objects so arranged together as to produce a group of seven—then we cannot believe in the existence of such a combination. Although people can allege belief in things which they cannot conceive, a clear conception is surely required for genuine belief. One can best understand Buchanon and apologists who argue similarly by pointing to the need for a sense of security that prompts the verbal formulas they call their beliefs. This need appears undisguised when he says that " 'saving' faith is . . . 'believing in' or 'believing on' the living Christ. Faith is an entrusting of oneself to this Lordship—and Saviourhood—of Jesus: it is trusting Jesus Christ for salvation" (p. 48).

Meaningless formulas give particular satisfaction when they combine others which are accepted as venerable and yet are felt to be unrelated or even opposed. T.F. Torrance confesses himself greatly impressed by Karl Barth's "doctrine of God as *being-in-his-act* and *act-in-his-being,* in which he combined the Patristic emphasis upon the *being* of God in his acts and the Reformation emphasis upon the *acts* of God in his being".[21] (The italics are Torrance's.) Alan Sell, whom we saw complaining of lack of deference to the theologian, himself complains of the "soteriological vagueness" of some of his colleagues (p. 45). It is admittedly difficult to write intelligibly about some of the traditional doctrines—about the Trinity, for instance, where the problem has always been to reconcile two opposite views: that God, Jesus, and the Holy Ghost are distinct, and that they are the same. A purely verbal reconciliation is easy enough and sufficient to command widespread acceptance, as when Torrance praises Barth's "doctrines of the *hypostatic union* between the divine and human natures in Christ, and of the *consubstantial communion* between the Persons of the Holy Trinity" (p. 123, with—again—Torrance's italics). Macquarrie allows that the wording of the traditional Trinitarian formulas perhaps "needs to be reinterpreted in the terminology of a more modern philosophy".[22] But so far as useful abstractions are concerned, most people have not enough ideas to go round the stock of words they use, and would be better employed in extending their knowledge than their vocabulary, especially as the new words are far too often introduced as the name of a mere pseudo-notion.

Macquarrie solemnly tells us, a few pages later, that

> My own way of expounding the triunity of God has been to see in this the movement of Being from its primordial source through its expression in creation to its unitive action in building up the kingdom of God. (p. 113)

Sometimes one can recognize some genuine idea behind pretentious wording of this kind, but then the idea is often trite or plainly unacceptable, and if expressed in simpler language would be dismissed as not worth making or obviously untrue. The writer is as likely to be deceived as the reader.

Those who acknowledge the inadequacy of their religious propositions sometimes defend them, as does John Bowker, on the ground that, although they are all provisional, corrigible, and frequently wrong,

> they may nevertheless be wrong (on many occasions of our using them) about something, and that 'something' then sets a limit

on language by being what it is, even though we can never describe exactly or exhaustively *what* it is. This is even true of something so relatively obvious as the universe. Truth can therefore [sic] be told in fiction as well as in fact, by way of poetry as well as by way of proof.[23]

The difference between ideas of God and ideas of the universe is that we can be quite sure that the universe exists, for we do know something, however little, about it, so that our imaginative constructions can proceed from some basis of fact. Graham Shaw has pointed out in another connection that it is only a similar basis that would entitle us to regard God as something like a relatively unexplored continent, maps of which can be made by conjectural additions to the little that is reliably known; whereas "if the concept of God does not refer to a reality which determines its content, but is a construction of the human imagination", then the analogy breaks down.[24]

In the type of writing I have been criticizing, the word 'concept' frequently occurs, and I may revert here to the theme of my opening chapter; for one gets the impression that the 'concept' is often understood—or rather misunderstood—to be something that combines the advantages of word, thought, and thing, while being free from the disadvantages of all three. It is definable like a word; it is constant and definite like a real object (not vague and fluctuating, as are mere ideas) and amenable to investigation in the same way; and finally it is abstract, like many ideas. The concept, so understood, is not like the concepts of physical science, such as velocity, acceleration, viscosity, valency, catalyst, and so on. In textbooks these are sometimes defined, but from a mere definition nobody would ever come to understand the meaning of the words. They refer to certain aspects of observable nature, and can be understood only when these have become familiar. In some cases they are amenable to mathematical treatment, but they can all be illustrated by practical experiments, ocular demonstrations. In some cases the term refers to visible objects or a class of objects; in other cases the objects are theoretical and only the effects are demonstrable. But even in these cases the theoretical part is representable in some material way, either by a model or a mathematical formula. These are the real scientific concepts, whereas the 'concept' that is so often mentioned in philosophical writing cannot be brought into any constant and intelligible relation with precise experiment or physical observation, although it can have a name. "What's in a name?" asks Shakespeare. The answer is: there is often taken to be a great deal in what is, in reality, no more than a name.

Notes

1. Words, Ideas, and Things

1. A.E. Taylor, *Does God Exist?*, London: Macmillan, 1945, p. 2.

2. B. Russell, *Human Knowledge,* London: Allen and Unwin, 1948, p. 200. Cf. Russell's *Outline of Philosophy,* London: Allen and Unwin, 1927, pp. 52–54. Further references to these two books will give simply date and page.

3. On Ogden and Richards, see below, p. 111.

4. John Locke, *An Essay Concerning Human Understanding,* first published in 1690, Book 3, Chapter 2, Section 5.

5. My quotations from Ayer are, unless otherwise indicated, from the second edition of his *Language, Truth and Logic,* London: Gollanz, 1946 (many times reprinted). For criticism of his views on language, see F.R.H. (Ronald) Englefield, *Language: Its Origin and Relation to Thought,* London: Elek/Pemberton and New York: Scribner, 1977, pp. 166–171.

6. Philosophy, says Ayer, deals in tautologies, and these "do not in themselves contain any information about any matter of fact" (p. 87). Their validity is "independent of the nature of the external world" (p. 84). The proposi-

tions of philosophy "are not factual, but linguistic in character"; hence "philosophical analysis is independent of any empirical assumptions" (p. 57). It is concerned not with facts, but with words and their relationships (p. 59). It supplies "definitions", the validity of which depends "solely" on their compatibility with linguistic conventions (p. 70). "The characteristic mark of a purely logical enquiry is that it is concerned with the formal consequences of our definitions and not with questions of empirical fact" (p. 57).

7. 'Logical Positivism and its Legacy', a dialogue with A.J. Ayer, by B.E. Magee, in the latter's *Men of Ideas,* London: B.B.C., 1978, pp. 130, 131. I acknowledge that Ayer's 'logical positivism' was based on profound dissatisfaction with practically all previous philosophy. Descartes, Locke, and Kant were similarly motivated, and C.D. Broad commented that, while they were largely justified in their criticisms of their predecessors, their own philosophies are equally vulnerable ('Two Lectures on the Nature of Philosophy', 1955, printed in *Clarity is not Enough: Essays in Criticism of Linguistic Philosophy,* edited by H.D. Lewis, London: Allen and Unwin, 1963, p. 42). Ayer's position is similar, and he conceded in his dialogue with Magee that *Language, Truth and Logic* is "nearly all false", although he still affirmed "the general rightness of the approach".

8. Dugald Stewart, *Elements of the Philosophy of the Human Mind,* second edition, Edinburgh: Constable, 1816, Volume 2, pp. 156, 164, 166.

9. Stewart criticises as "revolting" the view of a Mr. Leslie who, he says, held that "the whole structure of geometry . . . is grounded on the simple comparison of triangles; and all the fundamental theorems which relate to this comparison derive their evidence from the *mere* superposition of the triangles themselves; a mode of proof which, in reality, is nothing but an ultimate appeal . . . to external observation". Leslie added, so Stewart continues, that the ultimate empirical facts on which geometry rests "are so few, so distinct and obvious that the subsequent train of reasoning is safely pursued to unlimited extent, without ever appealing *again* to the evidence of the senses" (*vol. cit.* in note 8 above, pp. 199–200).

10. I have discussed the relation between mathematics and empirical facts in Chapter 5 of my *Goethe and the Development of Science, 1750–1900,* Alphen aan den Rijn

(Netherlands): Sijthoff and Noordhoff, 1978. See also chapters 10 and 11 of F.R.H. (Ronald) Englefield, *The Mind at Work and Play,* Buffalo, N.Y.: Prometheus, 1985. My discussion of Hume and Kant in Chapter 9 of my *Religious Postures* (La Salle, Illinois: Open Court, 1988) attempts (pp. 146–48, 160–62) a criticism of the commonly held distinction between 'necessary' and other truths. To that, I would add the following. Geometrical propositions are certainly more exact than our experience confirms. We cannot measure the angle in a polygon with perfect exactness, yet theoretical considerations tell us what the angle and the sum of all the angles will be. What has so often been felt as a problem is: if all our ideas of lines and figures are derived from experience, which is necessarily imperfect in this way, how can we deduce anything from them that is more accurate? I suggest that an answer can be illustrated in the following way. Experience informs us that, when two wedge-shaped objects are placed together, they form a new object, also wedge-shaped, but with a wider angle.

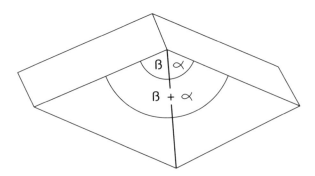

Experience further informs us that, if the angles α and β are both equal and suitably chosen, we can make the resulting angle straight, that is: two right angles, a right angle being defined as the angle which, when placed alongside another like itself, produces a straight line or flat surface (the idea of this latter being derived from experience of, for instance, the surface of a still liquid). We can produce a flat surface from right-angled blocks with such success that we may be unable to observe any unevenness, and we assume that any imperfections nevertheless present are due to our lack of skill or to defects in our tools. Since improvements in tools and skill are seen to reduce the imperfections in the results, this assumption is supported by experience. So also with other figures. The circle is a shape found in nature and easily made with simple instruments such as compasses. It was early discovered that a chord with the length of the radius is one side of a hexagon inscribed in the circle, although if we set dividers or compasses to the length of the radius and mark off with them the six points on the circumference, we shall probably find that there is a small gap or overlap. But if many such experiments are made, it is seen that the error is sometimes on one side and sometimes on the other, and this gives rise to the conviction that, if only the measurements could be made exact, the proposition could be demonstrated. In fact the more careful the measurements and the more refined the instruments, the smaller the error. Hence the conclusion.

When a number of general propositions have been established in this empirical way, it is found that one can be deduced from another. We can draw straight lines from the angular points of the hexagon in our circle to the centre and thus obtain six equilateral triangles. This tells us that a hexagon can be constructed by fitting six of such together.

That an equilateral triangle is also equiangular is suggested by experience and confirmed by experiment. We can fit an equilateral triangular tile into soft clay, so that when we remove the tile an impression is left. We then find at once that the tile may be replaced in the impression in three positions, each side of the tile fitting in turn against each of the sides of the impression; and as the sides fit, so must the angles. Thus we arrive at the result that, just as two right angles make a straight line, six of the angles that occur in equilateral triangles are equivalent to four right angles; for, having put six such triangles together to form our hexagon, as in the figure below, we find that the six apices that meet at the centre fill the space there without gap or overlap, and that three of them form a straight angle.

One may go on in this way to derive many propositions about angles, and the procedure is always the same: first an inductive discovery, then deductions which experience

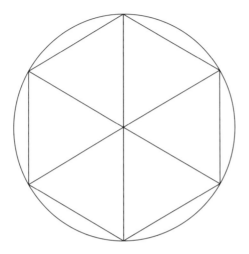

approximately confirms. The abstract propositions acquire ever greater prestige as this process of indirect confirmation continues.

Many philosophers have followed Hume in supposing that such propositions are necessarily true, whereas propositions such as 'there are kangaroos in Australia' only happen to be true. But as soon as it has been shown that this necessity exists only where we have been taught by experience to look for it, the whole distinction vanishes, and we may look for it equally between all kinds of experience. The propositions of geometry, made as simple as possible by the maximum degree of abstraction, depend on conditions which we can exhaustively contemplate, whereas the presence of kangaroos depends on a vast array of palaeozoological and palaeogeographic conditions, and if we knew them all, their outcome would appear to us as necessary as any geometrical inference. Hume believed that "the contrary of every matter of fact is still possible", because this contrary "can never imply a contradiction" (*Enquiry Concerning Human Understanding*, Section 4, *ad init.*). But the contrary proposition surely is in contra-

diction with the totality of the conditions, although it may
well seem consistent with any small set of them that we
may happen to hold in view.

11.

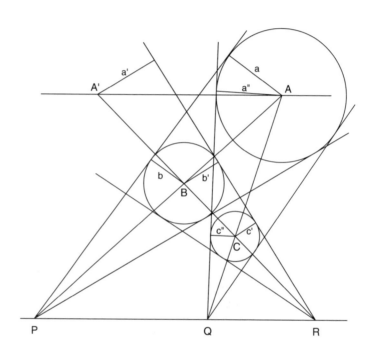

Join PR. It is then required to prove that Q lies on PR.
Through A draw AA' parallel to RP, to meet RB produced
at A'.
From A', B, and C draw a', b', and c', perpendicular to the
common tangent of the circles B and C.

From A and B draw a and b perpendicular to common tangent of A and B.

From A and C draw a″ and c″ perpendicular to common tangent of A and C.

Then a = a″, b = b′, and c′ = c″, since they are respectively radii of the circles A, B, and C.

Now, since AA′ is parallel to PR, we have:

A′R/BR = AP/BP, and therefore a′/b′ = a/b, and so a′ = a.

Then a′/c′ = a″/c″, and A′R/CR = AQ/CQ;

Hence AA′ is parallel to QR, and PR is parallel to QR.

Since R is common, Q must lie on PR.

12. W. Köhler, *Intelligenzprüfungen an Menschenaffen,* second edition, Berlin: Springer, 1921, pp. 80–84.

13. For Mill's arguments and a discussion of criticism of them, see my book on Goethe cited in note 10 above. Mill has a powerful ally in Ernst Mach, who shows that geometrical notions are empirical, and that even the irrational idea of $\sqrt{-1}$ was interpreted by means of geometrical applications of algebra (*Erkenntnis und Irrtum,* fifth edition, Leipzig: Barth, 1926, pp. 331, 421.

14. "Si l'on met sur une table une quantité quelconque d'objets solides et distincts, on *sait* que le nombre de ces objets sera déterminé indépendamment de la manière dont on s'y prendra pour les compter. Cette certitude est le résultat d'une expérience tellement ancienne dans l'histoire de notre espèce, qu'elle n'a plus besoin d'être vérifiée à nouveau expérimentalement pour s'affirmer à notre *logique.* . . . La légitimité de ces opérations est démontrée par une expérience sans cesse renouvelée et seuls ceux qui croient à l'essence divine peuvent éprouver l'impression qu'une vérité expérimentalement établie prend plus de certitude quand elle a été retrouvée par un raisonnement. (Félix le Dantec, *Les Lois Naturelles,* Paris: Alcan, 1914, pp. 48–50).

15. Ayer proposes (p. 53) not to speak of our 'ideas' of external objects and of our internal states, but to replace the word 'idea' by "the neutral word 'sense-content'." A sense-content is "an element in that which is sensibly given", "the immediate data not merely of 'outer' but also of 'introspective' sensation". What he means is this: the things which he has learned to recognize and give names to are known to him only as particular combinations and sequences of smells, sounds, colours, and so forth. They are, therefore, composed of the same raw material as his

'introspective sensations', by which he means, perhaps, his memories, emotions, pains, and pleasures. If he can distinguish one of his own thoughts from the thing thought about, it is not because of any essential difference between things and thoughts, but because the elements of the thing are different or differently related from the elements of the thought. He supposes, therefore, that it would be possible, if we had a suitable set of symbols, to describe both things and thoughts in a kind of neutral language which presented both kinds of entities on the same terms, as our familiar musical notation serves equally to record an opera and a hymn-tune.

In fact, however, 'sense-content' is no more 'neutral' a word than idea; for it implies the existence of senses which are affected by environmental forces, and therefore implies the contrast between mind and matter.

16.   Ayer, *loc. cit.* in note 7 above.

17.   C.K. Ogden and I.A. Richards, *The Meaning of Meaning,* fourth edition, London: Kegan Paul, 1944, p. 15.

18.   Bain says: "Perception is something added to the actuality of the sensation proper. It is, in fact, that element of the ideal that gets so mixed up or associated with the actual as to be the chief obstacle to our quoting sensations, purely and properly so-called. . . . There are many instances where a thing presented to the sense carries with it, in intimate fusion, ideas or elements not presented" (*The Senses and the Intellect,* fourth edition, London: Longmans, 1894, pp. 384–85). William James discusses the matter at some length in Chapter 19 of his *The Principles of Psychology* (London: Macmillan, 1901), and gives some account of the history of the idea of perception.

19.   "In writing a book", says Russell (1927, p. 44), "my own experience . . . is that for a time I fumble and hesitate, and then suddenly I see the book as a whole, and have only to write it down as if I were copying a completed manuscript". That he uncritically trusted this sudden illumination is suggested by his account in his autobiography of how one of his early philosophical works was written: "I arranged for a shorthand typist to come, though I had not the vaguest idea what I should say to her when she came. As she entered the room, my ideas fell into place, and I dictated in a completely orderly sequence from that moment until the work was finished. What I

dictated to her was subsequently published as a book with the title *Our Knowledge of the External World as a Field for Scientific Method in Philosophy*" (*The Autobiography of Bertrand Russell,* Volume 1, London: Allen and Unwin, 1967, 210).

20. Englefield, *op.cit.* in note 5 above, p. 139. See also Englefield's *The Mind at Work and Play,* as cited in note 10 above, pp. 39, 144–45, to which my account of the immediacy of many ideas is deeply indebted.

21. This view of the problems concerning appearance and reality is put in detail by Englefield, *op.cit.* in note 10 above, Chapter 17.

22. Spinoza gives "homo cogitat" (man thinks) as an axiom (*Ethics,* Part 2, *ad. init.*); but someone's conviction that persons other than himself think is in fact a theory— the theory that some internal process occurs intermediate between the impact of external things on their sensorium and their visible reaction to them. Keith Ward, as we shall see, repeats Spinoza's mistake.

23. K. Ward, 'The Step of Faith', in *In Search of Christianity,* edited by Tony Moss, published for London Weekend Television by Firethorn Press, 1986, p. 67. Further references to Ward which give only page numbers are to this article. References to his '1982' are to his book *Holding Fast to God: A Reply to Don Cupitt,* London: S.P.C.K.

24. On Xenophanes, see J. Burnet, *Early Greek Philosophy,* fourth edition, London: Black, 1930 (or later reprint), p. 122.

25. Alexander Bain, *The Emotions and the Will,* fourth edition, London: Longmans Green, 1899, p. 508n.

26. As one of many relevant Christian commentators I mention J.L. Houlden, who calls the historical evidence for the resurrection "complex, diverse, indirect and essentially obscure", and asks whether God would "make as much as is commonly claimed depend on a happening as difficult even to identify, let alone interpret". He is not impressed by the familiar argument that, if the resurrection had not occurred, Christianity could not have survived the setback of the crucifixion; for "there are instances of religious movements transcending such devastating defeats by way of the experience of new-born hope, not without similarities to that given by the resurrection of Jesus". I would add that the New Testament itself

(in the substance of Luke's Emmaus story, 24:13–35) shows how readily such new-born hope could be generated by representing the apparent defeat as quite in line with prophecy and hence in reality no defeat at all. Houlden, like other commentators, finds it quite possible to explain the origin of the resurrection faith without supernaturalism—as "part and parcel of a conviction that the last days, as foreseen in apocalyptic, were in process of realization and soon to be consummated" (*Connections: The Integration of Theology and Faith,* London: S.C.M., 1986, pp. 143–44, 152). I have gone into this matter in my *Who Was Jesus?,* La Salle: Open Court, 1989, pp. 38–43.

27.   Peter Medawar, 'The Phenomenon of Man', in *Pluto's Republic,* Oxford University Press, 1984, p. 245.

28.   Quoted by Pierre Leroy in his introductory essay to Teilhard's *Le Milieu Divin: An Essay on the Interior Life,* London: Collins Fontana Books, 1964, p. 38.

29.   Thomas Altizer, *The Gospel of Christian Atheism,* London: Collins, 1967, pp. 15, 23, 83, 88, 91, 102–03, 105, 107.

2. Behaviorism and Reaction Against It

1.   G. Ryle, *On Thinking,* Oxford: Blackwell, 1979, p. 33. Further references to this volume will give simply page and date. References to Ryle which give only a page number and no date are—except where otherwise indicated—to his *The Concept of Mind,* London: Hutchinson, 1949.

2.   K. Ward, 'The Step of Faith', as cited in note 23 of Chapter 1 above, p. 67. Ryle's book *Dilemmas* (Cambridge University Press, 1960) amply illustrates what Ward is here complaining of. Ryle there allows the physiologist the right to examine the sense organs and to inquire in what ways they may be impaired, but not the right to ask 'How do we perceive?' or 'Of what is seeing the effect?' For such questions could lead to the conclusion—quite erroneous, so he thinks—that "some . . . external happenings result *via* some other complex internal happenings in the special internal happening of seeing a tree" (p. 100). In

fact, he holds, seeing a tree is not a physiological process, nor even a psychological one, because it is not a process at all. 'See' is a word which "declares a terminus", like 'stop' or 'win'. "I can be looking for or looking at something, but I cannot be seeing it. At any given moment either I have not yet seen it, or I have now seen it" (pp. 102–03). He thus undertakes to determine what physiologists and psychologists may appropriately do simply by dogmatically insisting that the only admissible sense of the word 'see' is 'espy'. They are, then, not allowed to use the word as it is used by the blind man whom Jesus cured: "Whereas I was blind, now I see" (John 9:25).

3. G.A. Wells, *The Origin of Language: Aspects of the Discussion from Condillac to Wundt,* La Salle: Open Court, 1987.

4. I use the following abbreviations in referring to Chomsky's writings:

CL *Cartesian Linguistics,* New York and London: Harper and Row, 1966.
L and M *Language and Mind,* New York: Harcourt Brace, 1968.
CI *Current Issues in Linguistic Theory,* The Hague: Mouton, 1964.

John Lyons notes in the Preface of his *Chomsky* (third edition, London: Fontana, 1991) that "Chomsky's thought has not changed fundamentally at least since the early 1960s." For recent criticism of Chomsky, see Rudolf P. Botha's *Challenging Chomsky,* Oxford: Blackwell, 1989 (reprinted 1990 and, in paperback, 1991), and Amory Gethin, as cited in my next note.

5. Amory Gethin observes, in his commonsense criticism of Chomsky entitled *Antilinguistics* (Oxford: Intellect Ltd., 1990, p. 59): "If one attacks linguistics in general, linguists and others 'up to date' in intellectual affairs will very likely tell one that Noam Chomsky has, like Freud, changed the way we think about the human mind. Chomsky may have made mistakes, and may need to be revised, but he has opened our eyes to the fundamental importance of language and its place in our nature. But if one exposes the flaws in the Chomsky fundamentals, most linguists will immediately deny association with him. He is out of date, superseded". By 'linguists', Gethin means

practitioners of linguistics. He notes (p. 3n.) that it would be more appropriate to call them "linguisticians", as 'linguist' used to mean a person good at foreign languages, whereas practitioners of linguistics are "very likely nothing of the sort". Quite so. Many of them seem incapable even of writing intelligible English. Gethin's book is written from the practical standpoint of someone with long experience of teaching English to foreign students.

6. That speech is no more 'creative' than other forms of animal behaviour is cogently argued by Englefield, 'Linguistics: Science or Pseudo-Science?', *Trivium,* 9 (1974), 1–18. He notes (p. 2) that "it is the characteristic of intelligent animals, which depend at all times to some extent on trial and error, to combine their learned reactions in different ways under different conditions. Indeed, the same may be said of animals which depend mainly on complex instincts, like the hunting wasp. The wasp which seeks a caterpillar, stings it, and carries it back to the hole it has previously dug, performs this series of acts many times. But although we describe the series in general terms as if it were always the same, anybody who watches a wasp such as Ammophila will know that it must be different on each occasion. Each action of an animal which involves some part of his environment must be adapted to that environment in order to be effective, and if the animal moves about, his environment will in most cases change as he goes".

7. L. Bloomfield, *Language,* London: Allen and Unwin, 1935, pp. 28–30.

8. Englefield, *The Mind at Work and Play,* as cited in note 10 of Chapter 1 above, p. 33.

9. W.R. Brain, *Speech Disorders,* second edition, London: Butterworths, 1965, pp. 76–77.

10. Colin Blakemore writes: "It is almost certain that children would develop no language at all without continuous and lengthy lessons from an expert. There is in fact a *critical period* during which an infant's developing brain is able to master, by experience, the skill of talking. If he has no contact with speaking people before the age of about seven years old, a child will have the greatest difficulty in learning language later on" (*Mechanics of the Mind* (B.B.C. Reith Lectures, 1976), Cambridge University Press, 1977, p. 141).

11. "The human brain has a speech centre which is

an association area where ideas or memories, or rather the neurones which are involved with these, make connections with the neurones which control the speech muscles. What connections are in fact made depends, of course, on the experience of the growing child, and as long as the person can learn more words or phrases or languages, fresh connections can be found. But there is, I believe, no reason to suppose that this particular small region in the 'association areas' of the cortex develops to such a degree before other parts of the brain that grammatical rules are established before language is actually acquired. Yet this appears to be what Chomsky's theory implies" (Englefield, *art.cit.* in note 6 above, p. 8).

12.   I discuss Humboldt in some detail in *op.cit.* in note 3 above.

13.   Englefield, *Language,* as cited in note 5 of Chapter 1 above, p. 154. In this connection the distinction Chomsky and others make between 'langue' and 'parole' is of importance. It serves the purpose of permitting practitioners of linguistics to lay down definite rules for a language without having to take into consideration the way in which different people happen to speak. If this were not permitted, their whole theory would collapse, and so they understandably regard it as of great importance. John Lyons says: "the relationship between *langue* and *parole* is very complex". He admits that it is also "somewhat controversial" (*Introduction to Theoretical Linguistics,* Cambridge University Press, 1969 (reissued in 1981), pp. 51–52).

14.   John Lyons, *op.cit.* in note 13 above, p. 249. Unless otherwise indicated, subsequent references to Lyons are to this book and will give only the number of the relevant page.

15.   Chomsky, *Reflections on Language,* London: Fontana, 1976, pp. 83–84. Cf. Gethin's discussion of this passage, *op.cit.* in note 5 above, p. 156.

16.   Gethin notes (*op.cit.* in note 5 above, p. 169) that many of Chomsky's ideas "are the result of seeing language as an independent, self-contained, self-supporting system that has to be explained with reference to nothing but itself". G.P. Baker and P.M.S. Hacker observe that often even its verbal context suffices to make a statement unambiguous. They discuss one of the examples (namely the sentence 'Visiting aunts can be boring') frequently

adduced in support of the view that, to 'assign an unambiguous semantic interpretation' to a sentence (to understand what it means), we need access to information contained in its 'deep structure'. They comment: "If 'Visiting aunts can be boring' is a response to 'That old bag, Aunt Doris, is visiting us tomorrow', or a response to 'What a bore, I have to visit my aunt Doris tomorrow', it wears its meaning on its face, not in any 'depth-grammar', let alone in any 'mental representations' thereof" (*Language, Sense and Nonsense. A Critical Investigation into Modern Theories of Language,* Oxford: Blackwell, 1984, pp. 292–93). They also oppose the view that language is a "system" (p. 374). I take them to mean that, as I have argued above (p. 80), there is no systematic correlation between words and things comparable to that between the entries on a map and the actual details of a terrain.

17. Vivian Salmon, review of Chomsky's *Cartesian Linguistics,* in *Journal of Linguistics* 5 (1969), p. 166.

18. Descartes's view that animals are automata, and that human beings are also automata in a great deal of their behaviour, was based on his theory of the mechanism of the cardiac cycle, which he explained with the comment that, once we understand the motion of the heart and arteries, "which are the primary and most general movements that we observe in animals", then "we shall easily see what to think about all their other movements" (Fifth part of the *Discours de la Méthode;* a convenient edition is André Bridoux's *Descartes: Oeuvres et Lettres* (in one volume), Bruges: Gallimard, 1952, p. 157).

19. Translating what Descartes wrote in a letter dated 23 November, 1646, we find him saying: "Briefly, there is not one of our external actions that could convince anybody who examines them that our body is not merely a machine which moves automatically, but that there is in it a soul which has thoughts, except words or other signs made with reference to matters which arise, without relation to any passion". By 'passion' he means all those impulses and motives that affect behaviour except the 'reason'. The French original is given in Bridoux's edition of Descartes, as cited in the previous note, p. 1255.

20. Alexander George, editor of *Reflections on Chomsky,* Oxford: Blackwell, 1989, p. vii.

21. Lyons refers (pp. 314ff) to Russian by way of

illustrating 'aspects' of the verb, and implies that 'aspects' are a feature of verbs in all languages, though they are expressed differently. The word 'aspect' is used in Russian grammar with reference as much to the form as to the meaning, while in English or Greek there is nothing, so far as the form is concerned, that corresponds to the Russian aspects. Of course, the special shade of meaning which is conveyed by the perfective or imperfective aspect of a Russian verb must find some form of expression in other languages, but if the term 'aspect' is extended to all such forms, it ceases to have any grammatical significance.

Lyons also tries to base some kind of generalization on the fact that there is no one-to-one correspondence between the words of two languages. But this is no more than the natural consequence of the fact that languages grow up in relation to the needs and customs of the people who speak them. Nobody who observes the way in which new words arise and come into fashion today can see anything remarkable in this lack of correspondence.

In a later work, Lyons observes that, although "syntactic research of recent years, much of it inspired directly by Chomsky's work, seems to me to lend a fair amount of support to the adherents of 'universal grammar'", nevertheless "the results that have been obtained so far must be regarded as very tentative" (*Chomsky*, third edition, London: Fontana, 1991, p. 147).

22.   Otto Jespersen calls the grammatical object in sentences where the noun designates the result of an activity "the object of result", as in "he built a house, she paints flowers, he wrote a letter, the mouse gnawed a hole in the cheese". He says that this "class of 'object' . . . stands by itself and is of considerable interest" (*The Philosophy of Grammar*, London: Allen and Unwin, 1924 or later reprint, p. 159). But really, if we are going to take account of the meaning of the verb and of the actual relation between the verb and that which is called its object, then we shall have an endless number of different species of object: for example, object of emotion (he fears the dark, loves whisky, hates Henry), of exchange (he buys a house, exchanges his dollars, swaps some stamps), of defeat (he overpowers his assailant, beats his rival). One might go on indefinitely creating new classes of object as long as one could think of verbs with fresh meaning, and it is this consideration that makes nonsense

of the view that the grammatical relationship between verb and object corresponds to some real relation between the action and thing which the words signify.

Actions, processes, changes, movements always involve some thing or things which act or move, and very often the process cannot be described without reference to two or more different objects. In such a case it is common to have one word for the movement or change and another for each of the objects involved. Examples with one verb and three nouns are:

He knocks the nail into the wall with a hammer.

He washes the dirt from his hands with water.

He books a seat in the train to London.

There is obviously no common relation between any two members (such as subject and verb, or verb and object) of these sentences. The prepositions are determined by convention and the sentences would not be made unintelligible by their omission. Even when the same prepositions are involved, there need be nothing in common to the meanings; for the number of short prepositions available is small, and so each one must serve for a variety of meanings, as the following sentences illustrate:

He tore a hole in the carpet with his teeth.

He spent a day in the country with his brother.

He gave a display in the arena with his cycle.

23. C.K. Ogden and I.A. Richards, as cited in note 17 to Chapter 1 above.

24. James Mill, *Analysis of the Phenomena of the Human Mind,* new edition in two volumes, edited with additional notes by J.S. Mill, London: Longman's Green, 1869, Volume 1, p. 341.

25. See Adam Kendon's appreciation of Köhler in his 'Some Considerations for a Theory of Language Origins', *Man,* 26 (1991), 199–221. Cf. Mary Midgley, *Beast and Man,* Hassocks (Sussex): Harvester, 1979, pp. 229, 234.

26. Chomsky, *Language and Problems of Knowledge,* London and Cambridge (Mass.): M.I.T. Press, 1988, pp. 168–69, 183.

27. Otto Jespersen, *Language, Its Nature, Development and Origin,* London: Allen and Unwin, 1922, pp.

437–38. This book received its fourteenth impression in 1969 and is one of the most lucid and informative works ever written on the subject.

28. See my *The Origin of Language,* as cited in note 3 above.

29. Details in R.W. Westcott's review (*Language in Society,* 14 [1985], 127–130) of the symposium *Glossogenetics: The Origin and Evolution of Language,* edited by Eric de Grolier, London: Harwood Academic, 1983.

3. Magic and Ritual

1. Article 'Magie' in *Religion in Geschichte und Gegenwart,* third edition, edited by K. Galling, Tübingen: Mohr, 1960: Volume 4, pp. 596–99.

2. John Beattie, *Other Cultures,* London: Cohen and West; New York: Free Press, 1964, pp. 206–07.

3. I.C. Jarvie and J. Agassi, 'The Problem of the Rationality of Magic', *British Journal of Sociology,* 18 (1967), p. 60.

4. Wittgenstein's view of magic is quoted and summarized by John W. Cook, 'Magic, Witchcraft and Science', *Philosophical Investigations,* 6 (no.1) (1983), pp. 3–4.

5. D.Z. Phillips, *Faith After Foundationalism,* London: Routledge, 1988, p. 309.

6. Englefield, *Language,* as cited in note 5 of Chapter 1 above, p. 120.

7. *Ibid.,* p. 121.

8. R.P. Carroll notes that the Old Testament amply shows that magical powers were believed to be restricted to particularly gifted persons, namely the prophets, who were, in consequence, to be feared. "It was believed that the prophetic word had great power to achieve whatever it predicted. . . . The prophet spoke the word and things happened". He adds that "there are signs in the traditions that such magical powers were attributable to the prophet as the servant of Yahweh, so that it was the word or will of Yahweh that achieved some of these magical acts." And "the preservation of the prophetic traditions may have been due to a . . . belief in the effective force of the word

of Yahweh. For if the spoken word was a powerful force in the world, how much more powerful was the word of Yahweh" (*When Prophecy Failed,* London: S.C.M., 1979, pp. 58–59).

9. F. Le Dantec, *Les Influences Ancestrales,* Paris: Flammarion, 1905, p. 232.

10. Emma Hadfield, *Among the Natives of the Loyalty Group,* London: Macmillan, 1920, p. 96. The porpoises were addressed as follows: "Oh fish, I am truly delighted to see you, and I sincerely hope you are coming to pay a visit to our island. If you intend to come ashore, you can't find a better place than this. . . . I beseech you, come ashore here. . . .".

11. Plutarch, *Roman Questions,* 79, quoted by J. Lubbock, *Marriage, Totemism and Religion,* London: Longmans, Green, 1911, p. 130.

12. S.G.F. Brandon, article 'Magic', in *A Dictionary of Comparative Religion,* edited by Brandon, London: Weidenfeld and Nicolson, 1970.

13. A.C. Haddon, *Magic and Fetichism,* London: Constable, 1906, pp. 23–24.

14. Details of the procedure are given by E.E. Evans-Pritchard, 'The Morphology and Function of Magic', in *Magic, Witchcraft and Curing,* edited by John Middleton, Garden City, New York: Natural History Press, 1967, p. 6. A man wishing to increase the yield of the oil-bearing plant will pluck some of the grass stems (the *bingba*) and "hurling them like a dart will transfix the broad leaves of the oil-plant". One form of the accompanying spell— there are alternative wordings—is to address the oil-plant with the words: "You be exceeding fruitful, indeed as *bingba,* with much fruit".

15. S.J. Tambiah, 'Form and Meaning in Magical Acts', in *Modes of Thought,* edited by R. Horton and Ruth Finnegan, London: Faber and Faber, 1973, pp. 204, 213.

16. Englefield, *Language,* as cited in note 5 in Chapter 1 above, p. 127.

17. M.W. Meyer gives the following account of the mystery religions in his *The Ancient Mysteries: A Source Book,* New York: Harper and Row, 1987. "The mysteries were secret religious groups composed of individuals who decided, through personal choice, to be initiated into the profound realities of one deity or another" (p. 4). "Some of the mysteries seem to have developed from agrarian

festivals that celebrated the fertility of nature as it mani-
fested itself in the life cycle of crops. At Eleusis, Demeter
and Kore were goddesses of grain, and ancient agricultural
ceremonies dramatized the planting, growing and harvest-
ing of the grain. . . . Hellenistic devotion to the Syrian
goddess Atargatis . . . also emerged from earlier Mediter-
ranean concerns for fertility. . . . The Asian Adonis, the
Anatolian Attis and the Egyptian Osiris similarly were gods
who had died and who were linked to the life cycle of
vegetation, and the rebirth of fertility in the world of
nature is exemplified in the way these gods were por-
trayed. Myths about Adonis, Attis and Osiris hinted at the
germination of life in these three gods. . . . The development of early agrarian or fertility festivals into the mystery
religions involved, first and foremost, the conviction on
the part of the worshippers that the cycle of nature related
directly to human life. . . . Death came to all the divine
forces of nature—Kore, Dionysos, Adonis, Attis, Osiris,
the Mithraic bull—but finally life was victorious. Kore
returned from the realm of Hades; Dionysos vivified his
devotees; Adonis rose from the dead; Attis gave an intima-
tion of new life; Osiris reigned as king of the underworld;
and the bull provided life for the world. Hence if human
beings could assimilate the power that had made life
triumphant in the world of nature, they too might live in a
more complete way". Hence "joys for this life and hopes
for the next" were bestowed upon initiates (pp. 5–9).

Concerning the Osirian myths and rituals, Keith Hop-
kins notes that worshippers of the god mourned his death;
"when his body was mutilated and the parts scattered all
over Egypt, Isis collected the damaged parts together and
reanimated him; the believers rejoiced regularly at his
resuscitation" (*Death and Renewal,* Cambridge University
Press, 1983, p. 231).

Walter Burkert agrees that in the mysteries "there is a
sequence of mourning followed by joy". He adds:
"Firmicus Maternus describes a mystery scene in which,
after days of lament in the presence of an idol lying on a
litter, light is brought in and a priest anoints the throats of
the mourners, saying in a whispering voice: 'Be confident,
mystai, since the god has been saved: you too will be saved
from your toils.' It is unclear to which cult he is referring,
but it is evident that the fate of the initiate is modelled on
the fate of the god as represented in myth and ritual,

following the peripety from catastrophe to salvation." The overconfidence of a previous generation of scholars prompts Burkert to qualify this, saying that "there is a dimension of death in all the mystery initiations, but the concept of rebirth or resurrection of either gods or mystae is anything but explicit" (*Ancient Mystery Cults*, London and Cambridge (Mass.): Harvard University Press, 1987, p. 75). There is a certain sensitiveness on these matters because of their obvious parallels with Christian beliefs; cf. Chapter 8 of my *Did Jesus Exist?*, second edition, London: Pemberton, 1986.

18. B. Malinowski, *Magic, Science and Religion, and Other Essays,* Garden City, New York: Doubleday, 1954, p. 101.

19. J.A.T. Robinson, *Honest to God,* London: S.C.M., 1963, pp. 32–33.

20. Clifford Geertz, 'Notions of Primitive Thought', in *States of Mind,* edited by Jonathan Miller, London: B.B.C., 1983, p. 203.

21. G.E.R. Lloyd, *Magic, Reason and Experience,* Cambridge University Press, 1979, p. 2.

22. Cf. Cook, *art. cit.* in note 4 above, pp. 16, 20–21. H.J. Penner hints that it is because the beliefs underlying ritual (which he does not distinguish from magic) are so often erroneous that anthropologists have taken them to be mere expressions of desires and needs, not a means of fulfilling these—as if a theory which turns out to be wrong is necessarily something entirely different from rational adaptation of means to ends ('Rationality, Ritual and Science', in *Religion, Science and Magic,* edited by J. Neuser et al., New York and Oxford: Oxford University Press, 1989, pp. 15, 17, 24).

23. On Volney, see my 'Stages of New Testament Criticism', *Journal of the History of Ideas,* 30 (1969), pp. 151–55.

24. Pavlov's experiments with dogs are well-known, but the following brief summary may be helpful. A reflex is a stereotyped reaction to a specific stimulus, and a conditioned reflex is a habit based on a reflex. Given a reflex linkage between a particular stimulus (such as the sight of food) and a particular prelusive response (such as salivation before it is possible to reach this food) then a new linkage may be established with a new stimulus (for instance the sound of a whistle) provided the new stimu-

lus accompanies or precedes the old. When such a new stimulus has become associated with a reflex response in this way, it is found that other stimuli resembling it also have the power of eliciting the response. Thus a particular note A on a whistle, however carefully and exactly repeated in the course of the conditioning process, will be spontaneously *generalized* by the animal, so that other notes (A_1, A_2, etc.), provided they are not too remote from the initial one, become effective means of evoking the same response. If, however, the experiments are continued, and the animal is always rewarded with food after the signal A, but never after the signals A_1, A_2, etc., his reaction to these latter will gradually diminish, and so the two stimuli (A on the one hand and A_1, A_2, etc. on the other) will be discriminated. In this way, the original generalization is narrowed, and significant signals come to be distinguished from non-significant ones.

25.   Mary Douglas refers to an article by L. Marshall (in *Africa,* 27 [1957], 232–240) where it is noted that certain Bushmen "laughed out of court" anthropologists who suggested that their rain rituals had the effect of producing rain (Douglas, *Purity and Danger,* London: Routledge, 1966, p. 58). G.E.R. Lloyd comments that "the same article of Marshall's contains other suggestions about how the Bushmen do believe that they can control the weather, for example by cutting the throats of particular animals to bring in or to stop rain". Lloyd also notes that, although the rain dance does not aim at controlling the weather, it is not according to Marshall purposeless, but is part of ceremonies intended "to cure the sick and protect the people and drive away any of the . . . spirits of the dead who might be lurking to bring some evil upon the people" (*op.cit.* in note 21 above, p. 3 and note).

4. Language and the Bible

1.   John Tinsley, 'Christianity Direct and Indirect', in *In Search of Christianity,* edited by Tony Moss, London: published for London Weekend Television by Firethorn Press, 1986, pp. 31–33.

2. Ian T. Ramsey, *Religious Language,* London: S.C.M., 1967, p. 106.

3. Id., *On Being Sure in Religion,* London: Athlone, 1963, p. 89.

4. Id., *Christian Discourse,* London: O.U.P., 1965, p. 26.

5. I.A. Richards, *Practical Criticism,* London: Kegan Paul, 1929, p. 236.

6. D. Nineham, *The Use and Abuse of the Bible,* London: Macmillan, 1976, pp. 251, 259.

7. Jens Glebe-Möller, *Jesus and Theology: Critique of a Tradition,* English translation by Thor Hall, Minneapolis: Fortress, 1989, pp. 9, 26, 140.

8. John Polkinghorne, *Reason and Reality,* London: S.P.C.K., 1991, p. 2. Unless otherwise indicated, all further references to Polkinghorne are to this volume.

9. Id., *The Way the World Is: The Christian Perspective of a Scientist,* London: Triangle, 1983, pp. 50–51. This may be felt as some improvement on Leslie Weatherhead's position that the evil spirits prominent in both the epistles and the first three gospels may well in fact exist and be "the creators of things like some of the germs, bacilli and viruses of disease, the poisonous snakes and other organisms which seem the inveterate enemies of human well-being" (*The Christian Agnostic,* London: Hodder and Stoughton, 1967, pp. 187–88).

10. John Macquarrie, *An Existentialist Theology,* London: S.C.M., 1955, p. 170.

11. John Barton, *People of the Book? The Authority of the Bible in Christianity,* London: S.P.C.K., 1988, pp. 19–20, 61–62, 65.

12. David Tracy, *The Analogical Imagination,* London: S.C.M., 1981, p. 163. Quoted by Polkinghorne, p. 66.

13. Polkinghorne, 1983, as cited in note 9 above, p. 46.

14. Paul Avis, 'Apologist from the World of Science: John Polkinghorne, F.R.S.', *Scottish Journal of Theology,* 43 (1990), pp. 485, 495, 500.

15. Janet M. Soskice, 'Theological Realism', in *The Rationality of Religious Belief,* essays in honour of Basil Mitchell, edited by W.J. Abraham and S.W. Holtzer, Oxford: Clarendon, 1987, p. 108.

16. Polkinghorne, 1983, as cited in note 9 above, pp. 20–21.

17.   Thomas Ogletree, *The Death of God Controversy,* London: S.C.M., 1966, pp. 42–43.

18.   Keith Ward, *Holding Fast to God,* as cited in note 22 of Chapter 1 above, p. 120.

19.   On Jericho, see John Romer, *Testament: The Bible and History,* London: O'Mara, 1988, p. 69.

20.   Gerhard von Rad, *Holy War in Ancient Israel,* English translation, Grand Rapids: Eerdman, 1991, p. 53.

21.   "Most scholars agree that Jesus existed and that he taught, but what did he do and what teach? *Quot homines, tot sententiae. . . .* The old assumptions about the Bible have crumbled, and to a superficial glance only chaos has come to fill their place" (R.P.C. Hanson, 'The Authority of the Christian Faith', in *Theology and Change,* essays in memory of Alan Richardson, edited by Ronald H. Preston, London: S.C.M., 1975, p. 110).

22.   G.A. Lindbeck, *The Nature of Doctrine,* London: S.P.C.K., 1984, p. 122.

23.   Hans W. Frei, *The Eclipse of Biblical Narrative,* New Haven and London: Yale University Press, 1974, p. 16; *The Identity of Jesus Christ,* Philadelphia: Fortress, 1975, p. 144.

24.   Northrop Frye, *The Great Code: The Bible and Literature,* London: Routledge, 1982, pp. 60–61.

25.   Mark G. Brett, *Biblical Criticism in Crisis?,* Cambridge University Press, 1991, pp. 3, 6, 116, 143–44. This whole question is discussed in full by E.D. Hirsch Jr., *Validity in Interpretation,* New Haven and London: Yale University Press, 1967. He says: "A word sequence means nothing in particular until somebody either means something by it or understands something from it. There is no magic land of meanings outside human consciousness" (p. 4). "Meaning is an affair of consciousness and not of physical signs or things. Consciousness is, in turn, an affair of persons, and in textual interpretation the persons involved are the author and the reader" (p. 23). In criticism of Hans-Georg Gadamer's *Wahrheit und Methode* (published at Tübingen in 1960) he says: "To view the text as an autonomous piece of language, and interpretation as an infinite process, is really to deny that the text has *any* determinate meaning, for a determinate entity is what it is and not another thing, but an inexhaustible array of possibilities is a hypostatization that is nothing in particular at all" (p. 249). To this I would add that, if it is

impossible or unimportant to find out what an author really meant to say; if it is sufficient to extract mental nourishment from his words by the aid of one's own ingenuity, then it is not necessary that the author should have meant to say anything. It follows that authors will be encouraged to write—and students to read—what has no meaning. Hence the state of affairs prevailing in much literature and literary criticism today. In a chapter on "structuralism" and kindred phenomena (named as "post-structuralism, deconstruction, modernism, post-modernism"), Iris Murdoch complains that "literature written to please structuralist critics tends to be involuted and obscure because the objective is to *use,* play with, the language in a stirring, suggestive, puzzling, exciting manner. Traditional tale-telling or moral reflection or simple-minded referential uses of language are [from these premisses] to be avoided" (*Metaphysics as a Guide to Morals,* London: Chatto and Windus, 1992, pp. 185, 206). The theories underlying such performances are ably criticized by Ernest Gellner, *Postmodernism, Reason and Religion,* London and New York: Routledge, 1992.

26.   Kant supposed that the human mind is so constructed as to make certain notions, which he called *a priori* ideas, inevitable, because they belong to the very complicated receptor apparatus through which the soul perceives the world. What the soul perceives is partly due to this apparatus, and that part of the picture remains unaffected by anything that goes on outside.

27.   Maurice Wiles, 'Scriptural Authority and Theological Construction', in *Scriptural Authority and Narrative Interpretation,* edited by Garrett Green, Philadelphia: Fortress, 1987, p. 49.

28.   B.S. Childs, 'Response to Reviewers of *Introduction to the Old Testament as Scripture,' Journal for the Study of the Old Testament,* 16 (1980), p. 52.

29.   A. Kenny, 'In Defence of God', *T.L.S.,* 7th February, 1975, p. 145. Quoted by D.Z. Phillips, *Belief, Change and Forms of Life,* London: Macmillan, 1986, p. 20.

30.   B.S. Childs, *The New Testament as Canon,* London: S.C.M., 1984, p. 545. The unsatisfactory nature of Childs's position is clear from his discussion of the incompatible birth and infancy narratives in Matthew and Luke. He suggests that it is inappropriate to treat these two texts as "sources for reconstructing a biography of Jesus",

as this would not "do justice to the kerygmatic nature of the evangelists". The two stories, he holds, "are related to each other holistically", that is, they "are to be compared to each other in their entirety, and not according to their independent parts". He claims that the two do at least agree at their beginning and their end, and that this suffices by way of historical fact: "No additional historical information is needed in order for the two stories to function together within the canonical context. The inner nexus of the two sequences remains unsettled. The joint witness functions without having resolved the historical problem" as to "what really happened" in Jesus's early years (pp. 161–64).

31. Garrett Green ('"The Bible as . . .": Fictional Narrative and Scriptural Truth', in *vol. cit.* in note 27 above, p. 80) says that "attention to narrative offers theologians a chance to duck awkward questions about the *truth* of the stories" (p. 80).

32. D.E. Nineham, *The Use and Abuse of the Bible,* as cited in note 6 above, p. 234.

33. J.L. Houlden, *Connections: The Integration of Theology and Faith,* London: S.C.M., 1986, pp. 56, 94. Further references to Houlden in this chapter are (unless otherwise indicated) page references to this book.

34. Houlden gives these issues fuller treatment in his very lucid *Ethics and the New Testament,* London: Mowbrays, 1975.

35. John Fenton, 'Controversy in the New Testament', *Studia Biblica 1978,* edited by Elizabeth A. Livingstone (Journal for the Study of the Old Testament Supplement Series 11), Sheffield: J.S.O.T., Volume 3 (1980), p. 106.

36. M. Wiles, 'Scriptural Authority', as cited in note 27 above, pp. 51–55.

37. J. Barr, *The Bible in the Modern World,* London: S.C.M., 1973 (reissued 1990), p. 170.

38. Gilbert Murray, *Greek Studies,* Oxford: Clarendon, 1946, p. 67.

39. Barr, *op.cit.* in note 37 above, p. 25.

40. Daphne Hampson "cannot see what grounds there could be for using the word God if it were not that prayer is effective". She does not suppose God to be merely "a human projection" or "a construct in language", although "there is no need, necessarily, to think that God exists apart from humankind", and the word may perhaps

not "refer to a kind of entity, one which could be distinguished from all else that is". God may be "a dimension of all that is", for "much in science . . . suggests that all power, all reality is in some way in flow and interconnected", and "a realization of relationality and connectedness may well allow us the better to conceive how it is that prayer for another is effective" (*Theology and Feminism,* Oxford: Blackwell, 1990, pp. 169–173). From this—purely verbal—basis Hampson supposes herself entitled to question whether a certain fellow-feminist theologian whom she criticizes "has any concept of God at all" (p. 29).

41.   It has taken the experience of living for years in a society that has become increasingly multifarious in its composition and beliefs to bring a good many fair and liberal-minded British Christians even to the point of dropping Christian claims to a monopoly of recipes for salvation. In this connection, John Hick's recollections are of interest. He has recorded that, "for at least twenty-five years", the assumption 'outside Christianity there is no salvation' was "present in my own mind", although "I did not stress its negative implications". There is often such a gap between commitment to a form of words and imaginative appreciation of all that they imply—a gap which well illustrates how perilous verbal thinking can be. What seems finally to have given Professor Hick pause was awareness that, in a city such as his own Birmingham, there are "thousands of Muslims, Sikhs and Hindus, including deeply devout adherents of those faiths." This, in turn, led him to reflect that "the large majority of the human race who have lived and died up to the present moment have lived either before Christ or outside the borders of Christendom. Can we then accept the conclusion that the God of love who seeks to save all mankind has nevertheless ordained that men must be saved in such a way that only a small minority can in fact receive this salvation?". (*God and the Universe of Faiths,* London: Macmillan, 1973, pp. 100, 121–22). How difficult Hick's conciliatory stance is even for educated Christians fully aware of the facts to which he draws attention is illustrated when Adrian Hastings (Professor of Theology in the University of Leeds and Catholic priest) repudiates a Christianity that is merely "the appropriate folk-religion for the European West" and abides by "Christ's religious

uniqueness" and by the "ultimate universality of significance" of Jesus ('Pluralism: The Relationship of Theology to Religious Studies', in *Religious Pluralism and Unbelief*, edited by I. Hamnett, London and New York: Routledge, 1990, pp. 235–36).

5. Mental Adaptation

1. Ian G. Barbour, *Religion in an Age of Science*, London: S.C.M., 1990, pp. 189–190.

2. Hegel writes: "If it is correct—and it is so, no doubt—that man differs from animals by thinking, then everything human is human exclusively because it is accomplished by thought" (*Encyplopädie der philosophischen Wissenschaften*, Einleitung, § 2). Even if man were distinguished from animals by thought, it does not follow that he is exactly like animals in all other respects; hence it is not permissible to draw the conclusion that Hegel here draws from his premiss.

3. Evolution is nevertheless frequently invoked to explain cultural developments. For instance, an early reviewer of Jespersen's book on the origin and development of language (Edward Clodd, writing in the *Observer*, 5th February, 1922) declared: "On the evolution theory the matter is summed up in explaining language as a social institution which the need of communication between man and his fellows has evolved". The 'evolution theory' of the origin of anything is simply that it has evolved, and anything can be 'explained' in this way by merely asserting its evolution. Psychologically such an explanation is on a par with the older formula 'it was created', and those who are content to appeal to evolution would have been satisfied with this older formula, had they lived a few generations ago.

4. R.P. Carroll, *When Prophecy Failed*, London: S.C.M., 1979, pp. 101–02. Carroll is here summarizing the findings of Leon Festinger's *When Prophecy Fails*, New York: Harper and Row, 1964.

5. Englefield, *The Mind at Work and Play*, as cited in note 10 to Chapter 1 above, p. 55.

6. R.P.C. Hanson, *art. cit.* in *Theology and Change*, as cited in note 21 to Chapter 4 above, pp. 124–25.

7. Id., *Tradition in the Early Church*, London: S.C.M., 1962, p. 51.

8. N. Tinbergen, *The Study of Instinct*, Oxford: Clarendon, 1951, Chapter 3.

9. *Lind's Treatise on Scurvy*. A bicentenary volume containing a reprint of the first edition, edited by C.P. Stewart and Douglas Guthrie, Edinburgh: Edinburgh University Press, 1953, p. 59 (Part 1, Chapter 3).

10. See my summary of Pavlov's experiments, note 24 to Chapter 3 above.

11. Robert Runcie, 'Religious Broadcasting Today' in *The Canterbury Papers: Essays on Religion and Society*, edited by Dan Cohn-Sherbok, London, 1990, p. 8.

12. J. Macquarrie, *God and Secularity*, Philadelphia: Westminster Press, 1967, pp. 17, 108–09.

13. J.L. Houlden, *Connections*, as cited in note 33 to Chapter 4 above, p. 159.

14. Maurice Wiles, 'Miracles in the Early Church', in *Miracles*, edited by C.F.D. Moule, London: Mowbrey, 1965, p. 225.

15. *All God's Children? Children's Evangelism in Crisis*, a report from the General Synod Board of Education and Board of Mission; London: National Society/Church House Publishing, 1991, pp. 37, 54.

16. Dennis Nineham, *The Use and Abuse of the Bible*, as cited in note 6 to Chapter 4 above, p. 235.

17. S.C. Reif, 'A Jewish Response', in *Is Christianity Credible?*, edited by David Stacey, London: Epworth, 1981, p. 44.

18. Alan P.F. Sell, *Aspects of Christian Integrity*, University of Calgary Press, 1990, p. 6.

19. Houlden, *Connections*, as cited in note 33 to Chapter 4 above, pp. 112, 126.

20. Colin Buchanon, 'The Message of Salvation', in *In Search of Christianity*, as cited in note 1 to Chapter 4 above, p. 45.

21. T.F. Torrance, *Karl Barth, Biblical and Evangelical Theologian*, Edinburgh: Clark, 1990, p. 124. According to Torrance, to understand Barth's "profound integration of ontological and dynamic relations", we must "develop kinetic modes of thought" and operate, as Barth does, with a "dynamic" view of the inspiration of the Bible (p.

x). That "not a few people" (p. ix) have asked Torrance to write this book shows that this kind of exposition has its following.

22. John Macquarrie, *op. cit.* in note 12 above, p. 105. According to the doctrine of the Trinity, Jesus is fully God and fully man, yet genuinely one person. The only sensible way of treating such a 'conception' is to show how it originated—a task for the psychologist and the historian. It is admirably accomplished by Maurice Wiles who shows how, over centuries, the process was repeated whereby each doctrine about the nature of Jesus raised a further question about his nature, and that, of the possible answers, only one was, on each occasion, tolerated, others being vilified. He concludes that, for the Church, the overall result is "a well thought out but over-defined concept of orthodoxy", and "a penchant for mutual vilification and the multiplication of division, together with a built-in resistance to change in the face of new circumstance" ('Orthodoxy and Heresy', in *Early Christianity: Origins and Evolution to A.D. 600,* edited by I. Hazlett, London: S.P.C.K., 1991, p. 208).

23. John Bowker, *The Meaning of Death,* Cambridge University Press, 1991, p. 210.

24. Graham Shaw, *God in Our Hands,* London: S.C.M., 1987, pp. 36–37.

Index